MW00592638

Usborne

MY FIRST ENCYCLOPEDIA

Usborne

MY FIRST ENCYCLOPEDIA

Written by Matthew Oldham, Emily Bone, Alex Frith,
Alice James, Minna Lacey & Abigail Wheatley

Illustrated by Lee Cosgrove, Tony Neal & Jane Newland

Designed by Alice Reese

Contents

Our world

pages 6-37

From steamy jungles to scorching deserts
and deep blue oceans, our world is full of wonderful
places, plants and animals to discover...

Space

pages 38-71

Explore beyond our planet, among
speeding spacecraft, hurtling space rocks,
vast planets and sparkling stars.

Science

pages 72-97

What makes things move? How do ears hear?
Which things sink or float? Discover the answers,
and lots more fascinating questions...

My body

pages 98-129

Your body is amazing. Find out about your brilliant
brain, stretchy muscles, super senses and other
parts that work together to keep you going.

Animals

Enter the astonishing world of animals, from big, furry, fierce ones to tiny, shy, smooth ones, and absolutely everything in between.

Dinosaurs

Long, long ago, mighty dinosaurs roamed the land. Discover how big they were, what they ate, and why they aren't here any more.

Long ago

Voyage with Viking raiders, explore a bustling market in Timbuktu and meet the people who first invented toilet paper...

Index

Here you'll find a list of all the important words in this book, and where to find them.

Usborne Quicklinks

For links to websites where you can discover more about the topics in this book with videos, online activities and fun things to try at home, go to **usborne.com/Quicklinks** and type in the title of this book. Children should be supervised online. Turn to page 224 to find out more.

Our world

Our world, our home

From the *bluest* oceans to the *tallest* mountains, our world is full of spectacular sights. Wherever you live, it's outside your door, waiting to be explored...

Fishing boat

Ferry

Lighthouse

Cliff

Seas and oceans cover most of our world.

SPLASH!

Docks

City

CHUG CHUG!

Train

Most people in our world live in cities.

Farm

Moo

Cows

Coffee plants

Planet Earth

If you went up in a spaceship, this is what our world would look like. It's a big ball of rock called Planet Earth.

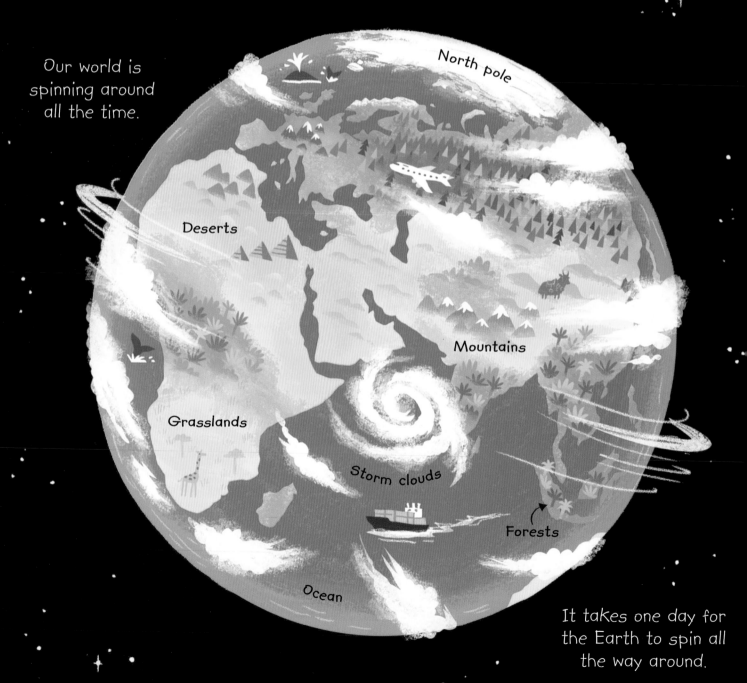

Our world is spinning around all the time.

North pole

Deserts

Mountains

Grasslands

Storm clouds

Forests

Ocean

It takes one day for the Earth to spin all the way around.

As it spins, some parts of the Earth catch the Sun's light, but others are in shadow.

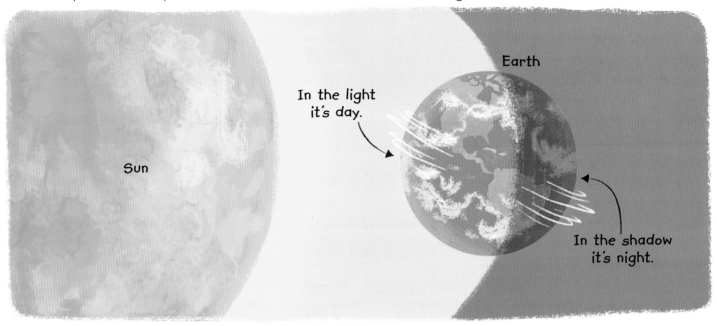

Sun

Earth

In the light
it's day.

In the shadow
it's night.

Maria lives in Brazil.

Fergus lives in Australia.

When it's day for Maria, it's night for Fergus.

When it's night for Maria, it's day for Fergus.

Changing seasons

Seasons are changes in the weather that take place at different times of the year. Some parts of the world have four seasons, others only have two.

In spring, flowers come out and lots of animals have *babies*.

Summer is the warmest season. Fruits and crops start to ripen.

In autumn, many leaves turn crimson and golden as the weather cools.

Winter is the coldest season. Some animals spend it asleep.

Earth is divided into North and South by an imaginary line around the middle called the Equator. When it's winter in the North, it's summer in the South.

Seasons change less near the Equator, where the weather is warm all year round. There's often a dry season...

...followed by a wet season, when it rains nearly every day.

13

Dusty deserts

Deserts are among the driest places on Earth and some can also be the hottest. Living things here have found clever ways to live in the heat, without much water.

Dried up soil turns into dust and sand that blows into big hills called sand dunes.

Falcon for hunting

Sand cat

Fennec foxes

This is an oasis, a small area of the desert where water is found.

Tents which pack up easily

Long robes to cover up from the Sun

Camels for carrying water and possessions

These people live in the Arabian Desert.
They travel around in groups called caravans to find food and water.

Hump to store fat for energy

Thick layer of fur to provide shade

Two sets of eyelashes to keep out sand

Narrow nostrils to keep out dust

Wide, flat feet for walking on sand

This is a camel from the Sahara Desert in North Africa. It can survive for a week without drinking.

Elf owl

Leaf-nosed bat

Burrowing owl nesting

This barrel cactus stores water in its fleshy stem.

Bark scorpion

Coyote

Rattlesnake

Gila monster

Tarantula

These creatures all live in the Mojave Desert in America.
They come out at night, to avoid the heat of the day.

Steamy rainforests

Tropical rainforests grow in parts of our world
that are warm and wet. They're busy, noisy places
where millions of animals and plants live together.

Vines

Pangolin

Parts of this rainforest
are so thick with trees,
people have never
reached them.

Red-tailed
monkey

Gorilla

Strangler
fig

Red river hogs

Albizia

Green
mamba

Grasshopper

Frozen poles

The North and South Poles are the coldest parts of the planet. The land and sea close to the poles are covered in snow and ice all year.

Research station

Albatross

People don't live on the South Pole, but scientists sometimes visit to do research.

Leopard seal

Emperor penguins huddle together for warmth.

Gentoo penguins

Killer whale

This floating ice has broken off a bigger block called an iceberg.

Weddell seal

The area around the South Pole is covered by a vast stretch of land called Antarctica. Most living things are found on the edge of this land, in or near the sea.

These animals have white fur to blend in with the snow.

Arctic fox

Polar bear

Arctic tern

Puffin

Reindeer

Walrus

Lemming

Both these animals live in water, often under ice.

Narwhal

Gelatinous seasnail

The area around the North Pole is called the Arctic. It's mostly covered by a frozen ocean. Many creatures that live here have a lot of body fat and thick fur to keep warm.

Parka (coat with fur hood)

Snow goggles

Mukluk (watertight boots)

The Inuit people live in the Arctic parts of Canada, Alaska and Greenland.

Some Inuit people build temporary shelters called igloos out of snow.

19

Mountain high

Mountains are the highest places on Earth.
They're *so* high, the weather at the bottom, or base,
can *be* very different from the weather at the top, or peak.

The coldest part of a
mountain is the peak.
Not many things live here.

**Mountain
peak**

Some mountain peaks
stay cold enough for
snow all year round.

Ski lift

Snow line

The higher slopes
are too cold for
trees to grow.

Over time, pieces
of rock fall down to
form a scree slope.

**Scree
slope**

Lake

Pine trees

When the snow and ice at the top melt,
they trickle down to form lakes at the base.

In winter, lots of mountains are entirely covered in snow.

In summer, most of the snow melts. Lots of plants and animals come out.

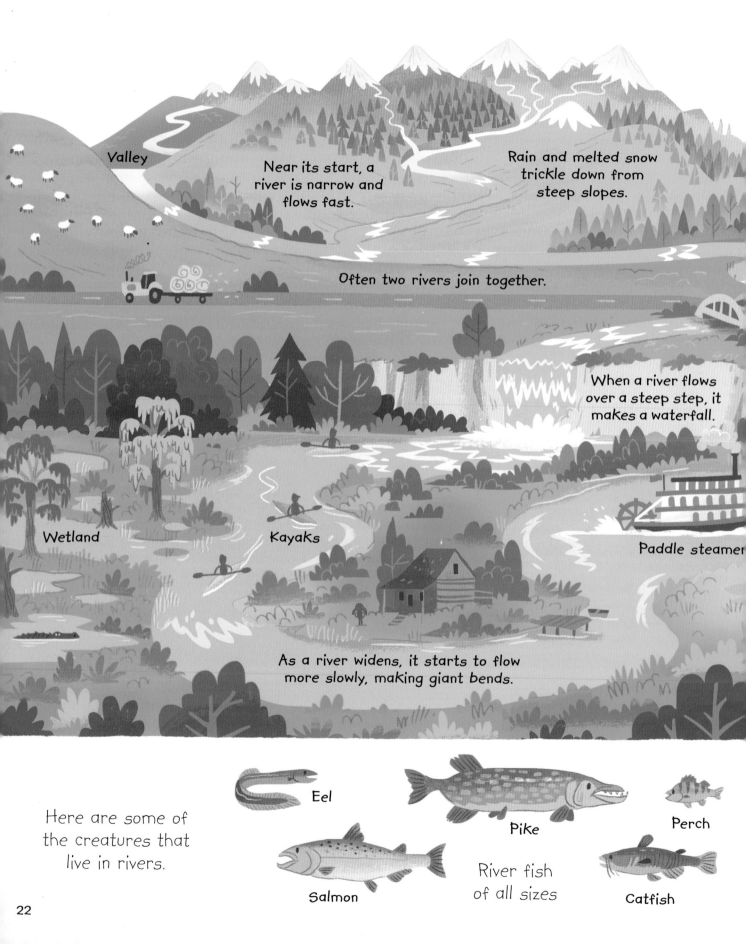

Valley

Near its start, a river is narrow and flows fast.

Rain and melted snow trickle down from steep slopes.

Often two rivers join together.

When a river flows over a steep step, it makes a waterfall.

Wetland

Kayaks

Paddle steamer

As a river widens, it starts to flow more slowly, making giant bends.

Here are some of the creatures that live in rivers.

Eel

Pike

Perch

Salmon

River fish of all sizes

Catfish

Running rivers

Even the widest river begins as a narrow stream on a hill.
A river always flows downhill, collecting more water along its way.
It ends when it meets another river, a lake or the sea.

Town

This river ends when it flows into the sea. This is called the mouth.

Reeds

Towards its end, a river can become muddy and shallow.

A river's mouth can be thousands of miles away from its start.

Pelican

Birds with webbed feet or long legs

Heron

Otter

Beaver

Animals with thick fur and strong tails

The coast

The place where land meets the sea is called the coast. Here you might find cliffs, beaches and all sorts of sealife.

Oyster

Mussel

Limpets

Scallop

Winkle

Clams

Cockles

The seashells that wash up onto the coast are the remains of different sea creatures.

Barnacles

Whelk

Crab

Starfish

Under water, sea anemones open their tentacles.

Seaweed

Sea urchin

Closed sea anemone

Pools are left behind when waves wash over the rocks.

When it's dark, lighthouses shine a light to show boats where the cliffs are.

Black-headed gull

Seagulls live and hunt close to the sea.

Nesting fulmars

Herring gull

Cliff face

Headland

Cave

Deck chairs

Lifeguards watch people in the water.

Crashing waves have helped shape these rocks.

Beach umbrella

When it's windy, the waves are bigger and more powerful.

Sailing boat

Seal

Lifeboats look out for other boats or swimmers in trouble.

Buoys show boats where it's safe to pass.

Under the sea

Most of the Earth is covered by salty seawater. Some sea creatures are found in the deepest, darkest parts of the ocean, but most live near the surface, or in shallow seas.

Scuba diver

Turtles

Jellyfish

Sea anemone

A group of fish is called a shoal.

Stingray

Brain coral

Lionfish

Coral reefs are found in warm, shallow waters.

Tree coral

Staghorn coral

Giant clam

Sea snake

Cone shells

Octopus

Crab

A quarter of all sea creatures live on coral reefs.

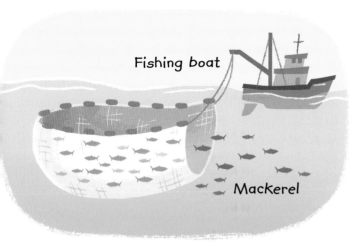

Fishing boat

Mackerel

The oceans provide food for people all over our world.

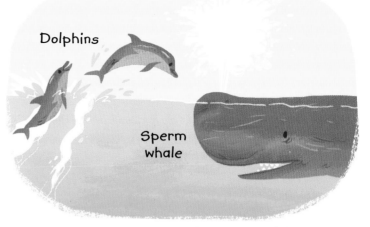

Dolphins

Sperm whale

Some sea creatures need to come to the surface to breathe.

Lion's mane jellyfish

Swordfish

Submarine

Manta ray

Whale shark

Hammerhead shark

Scientists travel in underwater ships called submarines to study sea creatures.

Black smokers pour out hot, dark water from under the sea bed.

Daggertooth

Lanternfish

Whalefish

Some of the creatures that live here are able to produce their own light.

Angler fish

Pelican eel

Parts of the ocean are so deep that sunlight can't reach the bottom.

Under the ground

The world beneath our feet is full of life
and buzzing with activity, just as it is on the surface.

Offices

Bank

Department store

Church

Manhole

Banks keep money underground.

Cellar

Foundations support tall buildings.

Sewers carry waste from toilets and bathrooms.

Pipes carry gas and water.

Cables carry electricity.

Road tunnel

Train station

Train tunnel

In parts of some cities, trains and cars travel underground.

Volcanoes

Volcanoes are openings in the Earth's surface. Sometimes the hot sticky rock that's buried deep underneath bursts through, causing a big explosion known as an eruption.

This volcano is erupting.

Clouds of ash

Hot gases

The red-hot rock that's forced out is called lava.

Blocks of solid rock

When lava cools, it becomes solid rock.

Lava

Some lava is runny and flows quickly.
Other lava is lumpy and flows slowly.

Over time, most volcanoes grow into tall mountains made from layers of ash and cooled lava.

Crops

Some volcanoes have stopped erupting. They're called extinct.

Ash from past eruptions makes the soil rich. Crops grow easily here.

Volcanoes under the sea can grow into islands that stick up above the water.

Earthquakes

The ground beneath our feet is usually firm and solid, but during an earthquake it can tremble and shake.

Most earthquakes...

...only happen in certain parts of the world.

...only last for a few seconds.

...aren't dangerous or even noticeable.

But some earthquakes are more powerful.

They can shake whole buildings...

...or even make them fall down.

In places where earthquakes happen often, people know how to prepare for the bigger ones...

Indoors, it's safest to shelter under a table while you hold on to it.

Outdoors, it's safest to stay in the open, away from *buildings* and *trees*.

Help!

Earthquakes at sea can cause giant waves called tsunamis. They can flow for long distances inland, flooding towns and ruining crops.

Wild weather

Storms look different all over the world. The most powerful storms don't happen often, but when they strike, they show the weather at its wildest.

In dry places, dust storms can blow sand for thousands of miles.

In cold parts of the world, blizzards can cover huge areas in thick layers of snow.

Tornadoes are winds that spin around very fast to make funnel-shaped clouds.

Some storms are so big you can even see them from space. They look like huge swirl.

34

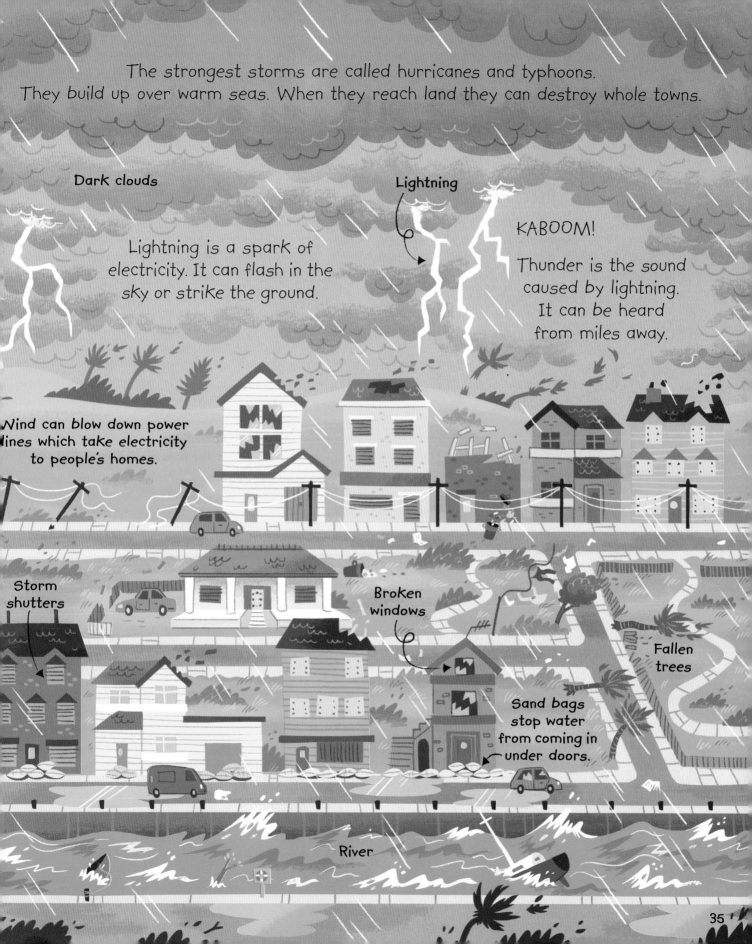

The strongest storms are called hurricanes and typhoons.
They build up over warm seas. When they reach land they can destroy whole towns.

Dark clouds

Lightning

Lightning is a spark of electricity. It can flash in the sky or strike the ground.

KABOOM!

Thunder is the sound caused by lightning. It can be heard from miles away.

Wind can blow down power lines which take electricity to people's homes.

Storm shutters

Broken windows

Fallen trees

Sand bags stop water from coming in under doors.

River

Living in our world

The Earth provides for us in lots of ways.
It has everything we need to survive, but we must
look after what we have so it doesn't run out.

We eat fish from the sea.

Most of our food comes from farms.

Drinking water comes from springs, rivers and lakes.

Metals and stones are used to make things.

Paper and wood come from trees.

Glass is made from baked sand.

Bricks are made from baked clay.

The Earth gives us food to eat and water to drink.
It also gives us materials we can use to make things and build houses.

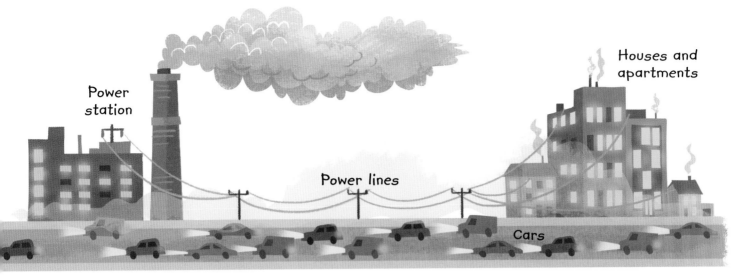

Power station

Power lines

Houses and apartments

Cars

Burning fuel gives us energy and creates electricity, but it can make the air dirty.
We also use some cleaner energy sources to make electricity.

Rushing water

Light from the Sun

Blowing wind

Small changes can make a big difference.

Pick up litter.

Recycle or reuse things.

Turn off lights when you don't need them.

Walk and cycle instead of driving.

Save water.

Enjoy being outside.

There's a lot you can do to look after our world.

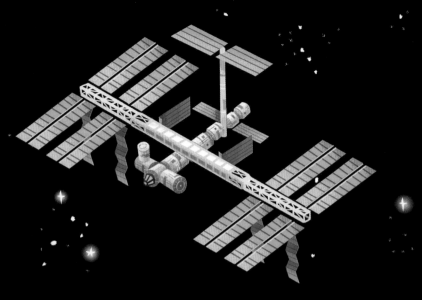

Space

The night sky

When the Sun sets, the sky grows dark.
You'll start to see twinkling stars. What you're
looking at is just a tiny part of SPACE.

Space is so
enormous, no one
knows how big it
really is.

Someone who studies
space is called an
astronomer.

The Moon is the brightest thing in the night sky.

This is a space agency, where people design spacecraft and train to go into space.

Rocket ready to launch

People who fly into space are called astronauts.

What is space?

We live on planet Earth. Space is everything around our planet. There are lots of incredible things out there.

Stars

Moons

Planets

Galaxies

Space probe

Space rocks,
called asteroids

TV satellites
send pictures to
your television.

Rocket blasting
into space

Comet

Earth is covered by a layer of gases, called the atmosphere.

This is planet Earth.
From space, it looks like
a green, blue and white ball.

The blue areas
are water.

The green parts
are land.

The Moon

The Moon is a big ball of rock
that travels around the Earth.

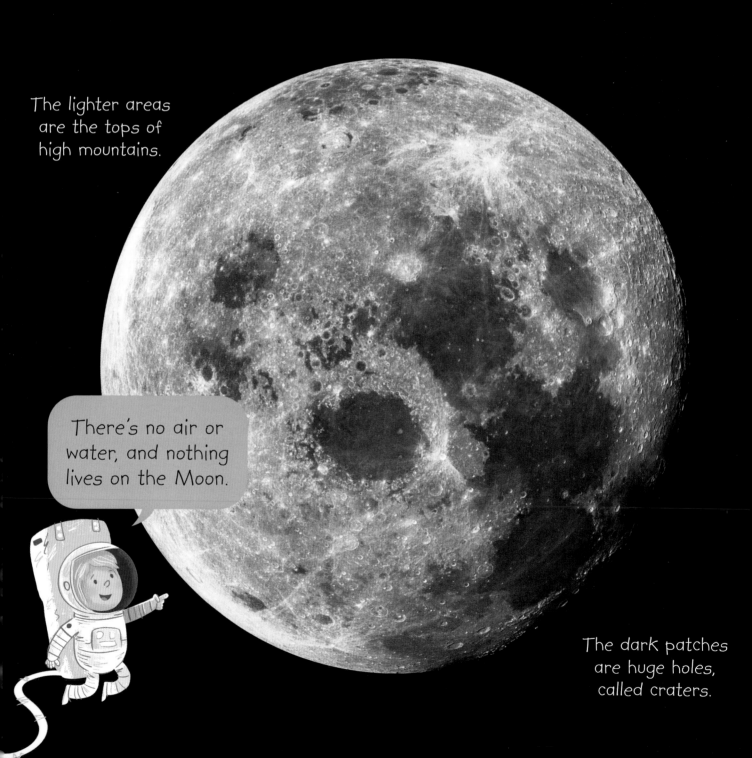

The lighter areas
are the tops of
high mountains.

There's no air or
water, and nothing
lives on the Moon.

The dark patches
are huge holes,
called craters.

Over 40 years ago, the first astronauts landed on the Moon.
So far, only 12 astronauts have ever been there.

The first astronauts on the Moon left a flag to show they had visited.

Lunar module

Filming

Collecting Moon rocks

Space suit

Moon buggy

Space school

Before astronauts go into space,
they have to do a lot of training.

Learning everything about
space and space travel

Getting very fit and
being tested on it

Finding out how to work
spacecraft controls

Emergency
escape drills

Learning what to do if
they crash into the sea

Using tools

Learning the languages of
astronauts from different countries

Repairing a pretend spacecraft
while floating in a huge water tank

Talking to experienced
astronauts

Being given a mission and
meeting the rest of the crew

Lift-off!

A rocket, called a launch vehicle, flies
a team of three astronauts into space.

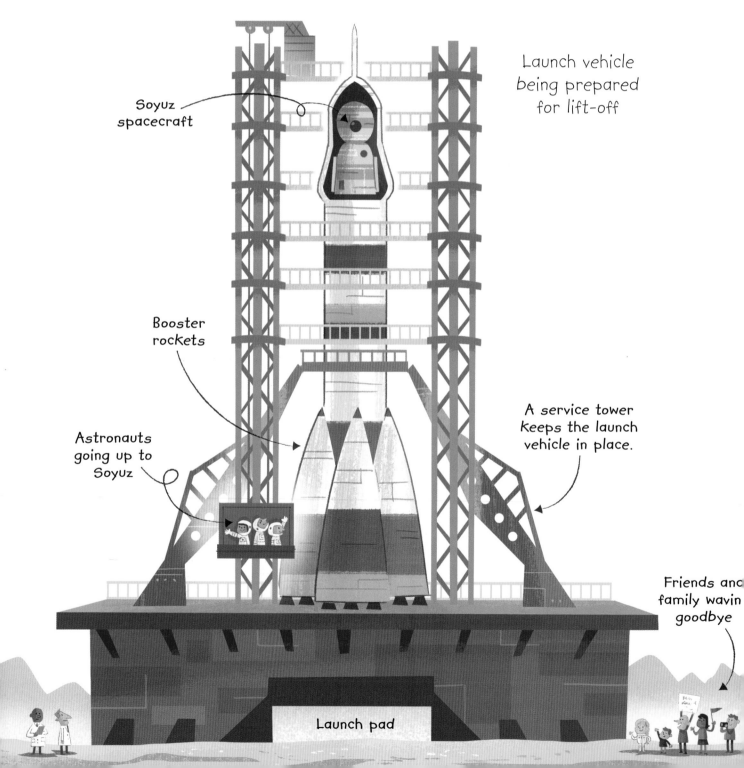

Soyuz
spacecraft

Launch vehicle
being prepared
for lift-off

Booster
rockets

A service tower
keeps the launch
vehicle in place.

Astronauts
going up to
Soyuz

Friends and
family waving
goodbye

Launch pad

Astronauts inside Soyuz
getting ready for lift-off

Booster rockets firing

LIFT-OFF!

Booster rockets falling
back to Earth

Launch vehicle falling back
and Soyuz flying away

Space station

In space, astronauts live and work in a spacecraft called the International Space Station. It flies high above the Earth.

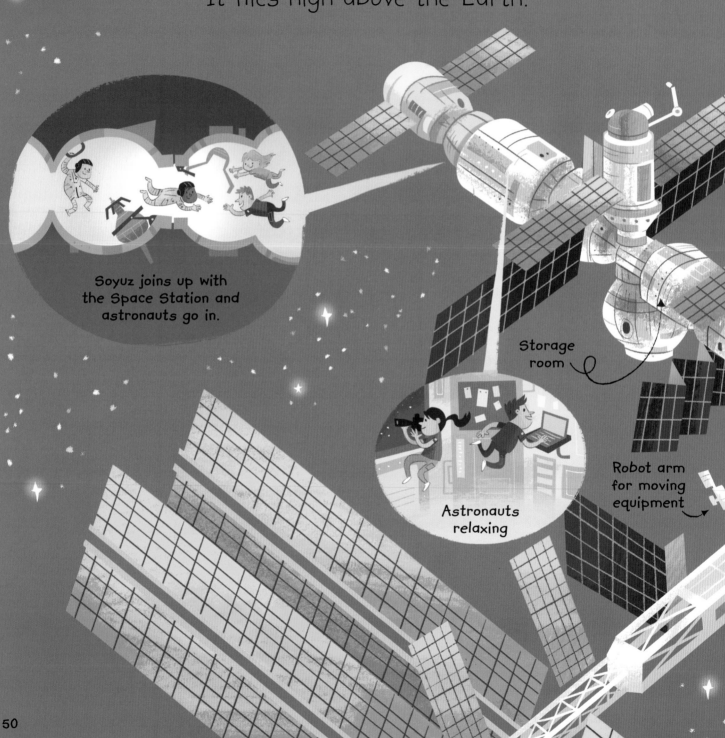

Soyuz joins up with the Space Station and astronauts go in.

Astronauts relaxing

Storage room

Robot arm for moving equipment

Living in space

On the Space Station, everything floats.
This is what happens during a day:

Washing using
dry shampoo

Using the toilet

Exercising for two hours

Most food
comes in
packets.

Eating

Repairing the outside of
the Space Station

Doing experiments

Relaxing

Cleaning

Receiving deliveries from
supply spacecraft

Unpacking supplies

Talking to family back home

Taking photos of Earth

Going to sleep

Spacewalk

There's no air in space. When astronauts go on a spacewalk outside the Space Station, they have to wear a space suit that gives them air and keeps them safe.

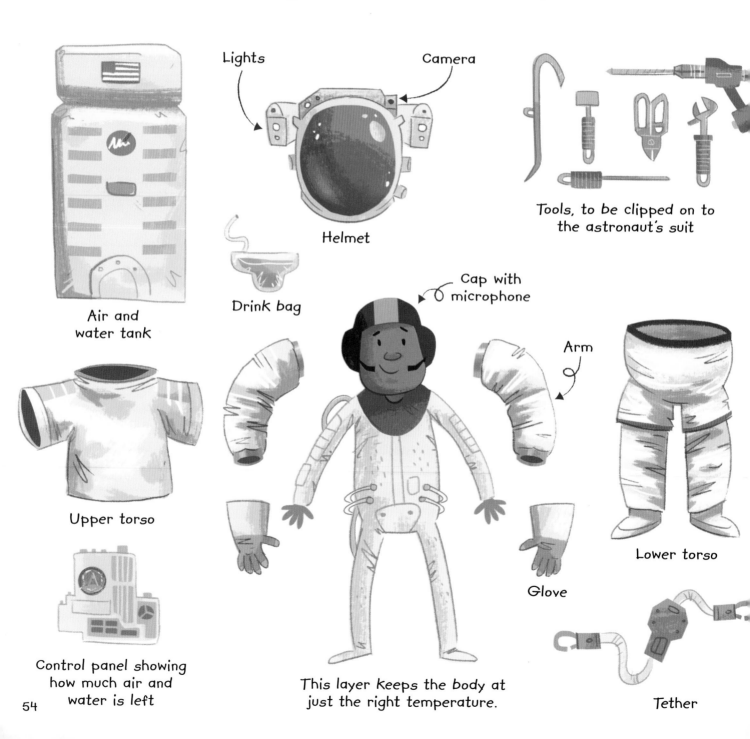

Air and water tank

Lights

Camera

Helmet

Tools, to be clipped on to the astronaut's suit

Drink bag

Upper torso

Cap with microphone

Arm

Glove

Lower torso

Control panel showing how much air and water is left

This layer keeps the body at just the right temperature.

Tether

54

Astronauts go on spacewalks in pairs.

Checking spacesuits and putting them on

Going into an airlock for 24 hours

Opening the exit hatch

Attaching the tether and going outside

Receiving instructions from Earth

Fitting new equipment to the Space Station

Drinking from the drink bag

Returning to the Space Station

The Solar System

The Earth is one of eight planets that travel around the Sun. The Sun and the planets are known as the Solar System.

Mercury

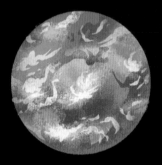

Earth

This is the Moo
Other planets
have moons, to

The Sun

Sometimes, space rocks
crash into planets.

Venus

Venus is
covered in thick,
poisonous clouds.

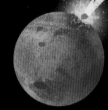

Mars

Jupiter

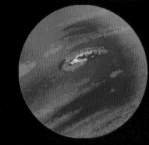

Jupiter, Saturn, Uranus and Neptune aren't solid. They're balls of gas or liquid.

Neptune

The Great Red Spot is a huge storm.

Jupiter is the biggest planet. It has more than 60 moons.

A comet is a ball of gas, ice and dust.

Uranus

It leaves a bright tail behind it.

Uranus has rings made from ice and dust.

The Asteroid Belt is a big group of space rocks.

This is Pluto. It's a dwarf planet.

Saturn

Saturn's rings are made from chunks of rock and ice.

Exploring Mars

Small spacecraft have flown vehicles, called rovers, to Mars. Rovers find out more about the rocks and air on Mars.

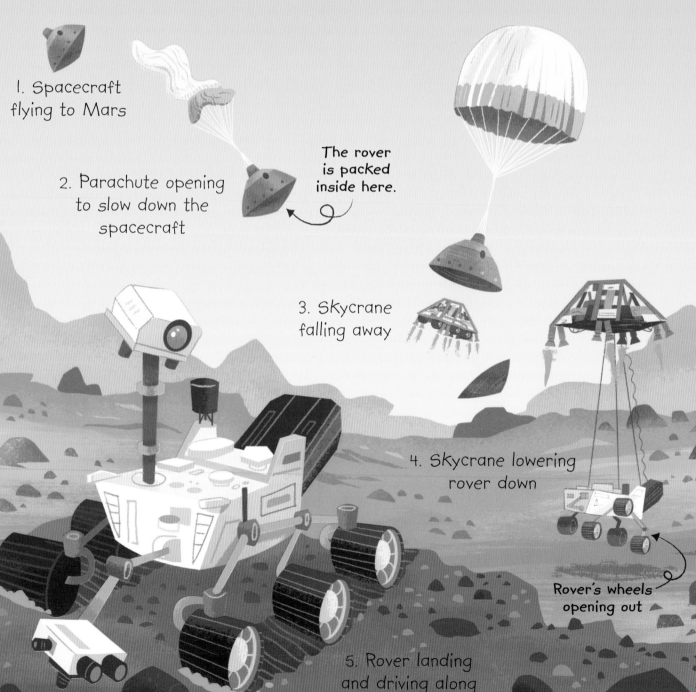

1. Spacecraft flying to Mars

2. Parachute opening to slow down the spacecraft

The rover is packed inside here.

3. Skycrane falling away

4. Skycrane lowering rover down

Rover's wheels opening out

5. Rover landing and driving along

Receiving instructions
from Earth

Exploring different places
and taking pictures

Firing a laser and drilling into rocks
to find out what's inside them

Scooping up dust
and testing it

Finding out about the
weather on Mars

Sending pictures
back to Earth

Stars

Stars are massive balls of very, very hot gases.
The Sun is a star. This is what it looks like close up.

Gases bubbling on
the Sun's surface

This is a solar
flare, a big
explosion.

From Earth, the Sun
looks bigger than
other stars because
it's our closest star.

There are different types of stars.

Our Sun is a type
of star called a
yellow dwarf.

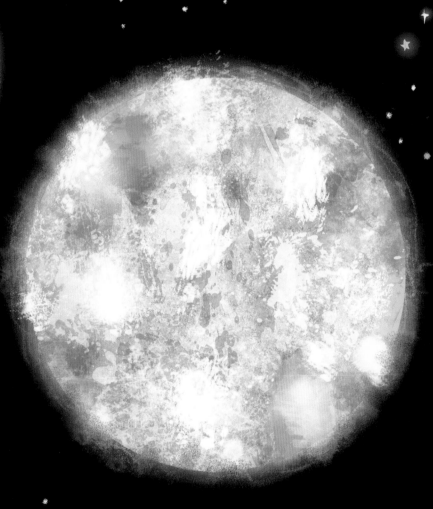

The biggest and most
powerful stars are
called supergiants.

The least powerful
stars are called
red dwarfs.

Life of a star

A new star is formed out of a huge, swirling cloud of gas and dust called a nebula.

This is the
Tarantula Nebula.

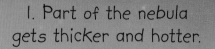

1. Part of the nebula
gets thicker and hotter.

2. Slowly, it turns
into a hot ball.

3. This becomes
a new star.

Stars glow and burn for millions and millions of years.
Then, they start to change.

Different stars change in different ways.

1. A yellow dwarf star gets cooler, bigger and duller.

2. Its outer layers puff away.

3. Eventually, a white dwarf star is left behind.

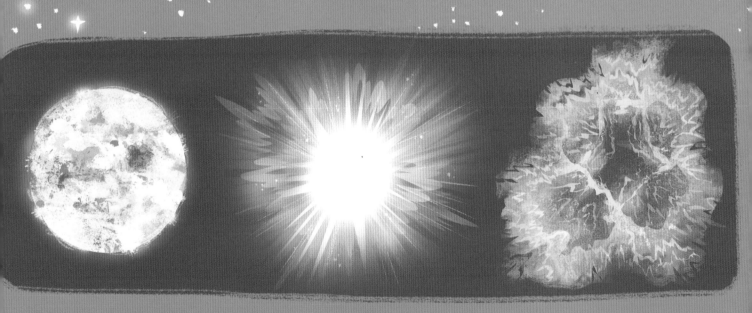

1. A supergiant star gets bigger and brighter.

2. It explodes. This is called a supernova.

3. A big cloud of gas is left behind.

Great galaxies

Millions and millions of stars form massive groups, called galaxies. Galaxies come in different shapes and sizes.

This is a spiral galaxy.

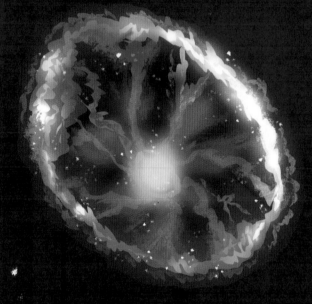

This is called the Cartwheel Galaxy, because it looks like a wheel.

Some galaxies look like bright balls.

Other galaxies are slowly joining together.

Looking at space

Telescopes help people to see things in space that are very far away. There are lots of different types.

Space telescopes take pictures of things in space.

Probes fly around planets.

Hubble Space Telescope

Optical telescope

Radio telescopes look for faraway stars and galaxies.

Mirrors make things look bigger.

With telescopes or binoculars you can see things in more detail.

Hubble is a famous space telescope.

A spacecraft taking Hubble into space

Hubble flying around the Earth

Astronauts have been sent to make repairs.

Radio dishes on Earth collect the pictures, then send them to computers.

Astronauts fitting new cameras onto Hubble

Hubble taking lots of pictures and sending them back to Earth

Each swirl and dot in this picture is a faraway galaxy.

Scientists studying the pictures

Stargazing

The best time to see stars is on a cloudless
night when the moon isn't too bright.

It can *be* cold at night, *so* wrap up warm. It's more comfortable
if you lie or sit on a blanket. Bring snacks and hot drinks.

Stars look like tiny points
of light in the sky.

But really they're huge
balls of fire, like the Sun.

The Sun is the closest star.
Other stars are very far awa~

Some of the things shining in the night *sky* aren't stars at all.

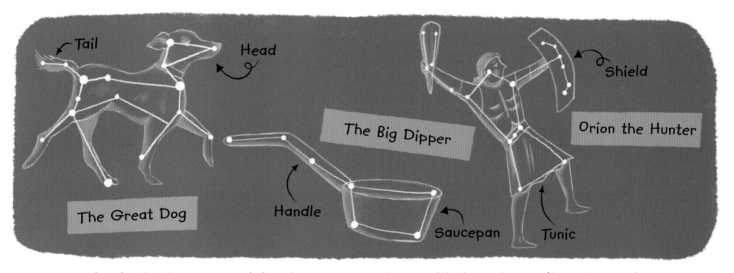

Ancient stargazers joined up some stars with imaginary lines to make pictures called constellations. These are just a few of them.

What you can *see* in the *sky* depends on where you are and what time of year it is.

Moon watching

The Moon is usually easy to spot in the night sky, but it looks different at different times. If you look carefully, you can see pale and dark patches on its surface.

When the Moon looks like this, it's called a Full Moon.

These pale spots are holes known as craters.

These dark patches are called seas, but really they're smooth rock.

You can get a good view of the Moon through binoculars or a telescope.

New Moon

The Moon looks different at different times.
Over a month, it goes from a New Moon to
a Full Moon, and back again.

Full Moon

When the Moon is
close to the horizon, it
sometimes looks yellow.

On cold nights you can
sometimes see a pale
ring around the Moon.

When the Moon shines
brightly, it makes
shadows on the ground.

Science

What is science?

Science is about the world around us.
It teaches us about nearly everything –
from what goes on inside our bodies,
to the air we breathe, to faraway planets.

People who study science
are called scientists.

What do
magnets do?

How do
they work?

Their work often
starts with lots
of questions.

Next they think
of ideas about how
to answer these
questions.

The magnet
only picks up
the fork.

Then they try out the ideas by
doing tests called experiments.

This is a laboratory,
a room where
scientists carry out
experiments.

74

When they do experiments, scientists watch what happens very carefully, and write it down.

They often use tools to help them measure what happens and see things clearly.

A microscope is a tool that helps people see very small things.

A stopwatch is used to time things.

A magnifying glass makes things look bigger.

Which one will sink faster?

A ruler is used to measure size.

There are many different types of scientists.

Some scientists study living things such as plants and people.

Some study what things are made of – and what might make them change.

Some study how and why things move.

75

Light and dark

Different things make light.
Without it, people wouldn't be able to
see and everything would be DARK.

During the day the Sun
lights up the world.

At night, twinkling stars
shine in the sky.

Candles

Fire

When things burn,
they give us light.

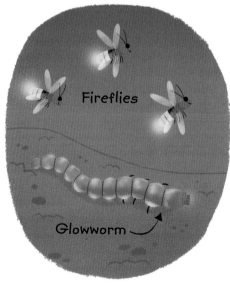

Fireflies

Glowworm

Some living things can
make their own light.

Lamp

Phone

People can use electricity
to make light, too.

When an object blocks out light, it makes a shadow.

If the object moves closer to the light, the shadow becomes bigger and fuzzier.

The Sun makes a rainbow when it shines through drops of water.

When the Sun shines through rain, a big rainbow can appear in the sky.

Reflections happen when light hits something shiny and bounces off it again.

Sounds all around

There are many different sounds in the world around you. You hear sounds when they reach your ears.

There are lots of ways you can make sounds.

You can use your body.

CLAP

OOoo

You can blow on things.

PEEP

CLICK

RATATAT

You can scrape things.

DURRR

JINGLE

CHING

You can shake things.

THWACK

You can hit things.

RATTLE

BANG

TING

There are
quiet sounds...

and there are
loud sounds.

If a sound is very loud,
you might feel it buzzing.

Sounds grow louder and louder
as you get closer to them.

Sometimes you can hear a sound
before you see what's made it.

Sounds happen when something
makes the air wobble.

The air wobbles a tiny
bone inside your ear.

Your brain recognizes
the wobbling as a sound.

79

Air everywhere

Air is all around us. You can't see it,
but sometimes you can feel it.

You can feel air when
you breathe out.

When the wind blows,
you can feel rushing air.

You can also feel rushing air
if you move quickly.

Some things can float in air. These balloons are filled with something called helium.
Helium is lighter than air. That makes the balloons float.

When things fall to the ground,
the air rushes past them.

Some things catch the air as they fall.
This makes them fall more slowly.

These sails catch the air when the wind blows.
This pushes the boats along.

Paper planes can glide through the air.

Mine has big, wide wings so it stays in the air for longer.

The bigger and flatter something is, the more air it can catch.

What are things made of?

Everything in the world is made from
different types of stuff called materials.
Different materials can do different things.

Some types of materials are hard.

Some types of materials are soft.

Some types of materials are light.

Some types of materials are heavy.

Some types of materials can stretch or bend, but others are stiff.

Some types of materials
soak up water.

Some types of materials
keep water out.

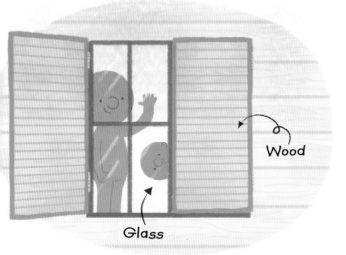

Some types of materials are
see-through, and some aren't.

Many materials
we use come from
the natural world,
but some, such as
plastic, are made
by people.

Floating and sinking

When you put different materials in water, some of them float near the top, and some of them sink to the bottom.

Apple

Paper clips

Pebbles

Metal key

Cork

Full glass bottle

Empty glass bottle

Which of these things do you think will float?

Metal fork

Glass marble

Clay pot

Shells

Paper straw

Tennis ball

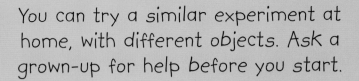
You can try a similar experiment at home, with different objects. Ask a grown-up for help before you start.

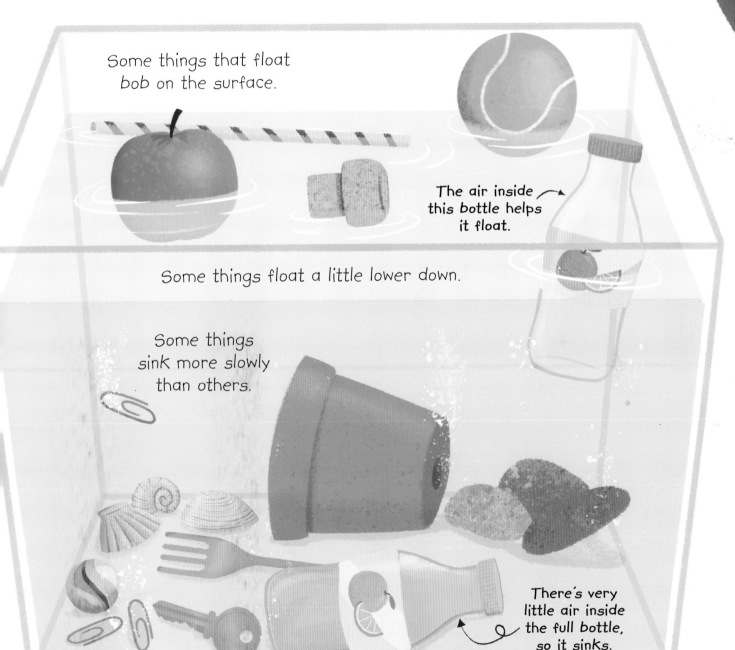

Some things that float bob on the surface.

The air inside this bottle helps it float.

Some things float a little lower down.

Some things sink more slowly than others.

There's very little air inside the full bottle, so it sinks.

How things change

Materials can change. Sometimes they can change when they're mixed with other materials. Sometimes they can change if they get hot or cold.

Mixing two different materials can make them change.

Sugar

Sugar disappears when it mixes with water.

Water

Soap

Soap mixes with water to make a bubbly foam.

Water

Cream

You can make cream fluffy by mixing air into it with a whisk.

Water

Powdery flour mixes with water and other ingredients to make dough.

Flour

Oil

Vinegar

Some things don't mix together easily. The oil in salad dressing floats on top of the vinegar.

Some materials change if you heat them up
but change *back* again when they cool down.

Some materials change if you cool them down
but change *back* again when they warm up.

Some materials change if you heat them up,
and they don't change *back* – even when they cool down.

The world of plants

Plants are living things that come in many shapes and sizes – from swishing grasses and tangled bushes to enormous, towering trees.

Plants need air, water and sunlight to grow.

Leaves soak up sunlight. They use energy from the Sun to make food.

Some leaves are wide and flat.

Some leaves look like spiky needles or sharp scales.

Nearly all plants have roots that grow down into the ground.

How a seed grows

Many plants grow from tiny seeds. This is a sunflower seed.

The seed cracks. A tiny root appears.

A shoot pushes above the soil and leaves sprout.

Most plants grow flowers.

Branches

Nuts

Flowers make fruits.

Fruits contain seeds.

Tree trunk

Flowers

Some fruits are dry and hard, such as nuts.

Some fruits are soft and juicy.

Berries

Roots

Roots keep plants firmly in the ground.

Roots also suck up water from the soil.

The plant grows bigger. More leaves and a flower bud appear.

The flower opens and seeds form in the middle.

The flower fades. Seeds fall to the ground, ready to grow again.

Trees and leaves

Trees and their leaves grow in many shapes and sizes.

Poplar

Oak

Cedar

Some trees are tall and thin...

some have wide spreading branches...

and some have a pointed shape.

Birch

Trees that lose all their leaves in winter are called deciduous.

Eucalyptus

Trees that keep their leaves all year are called evergreen.

Apple trees are deciduous. This is how they change through the year.

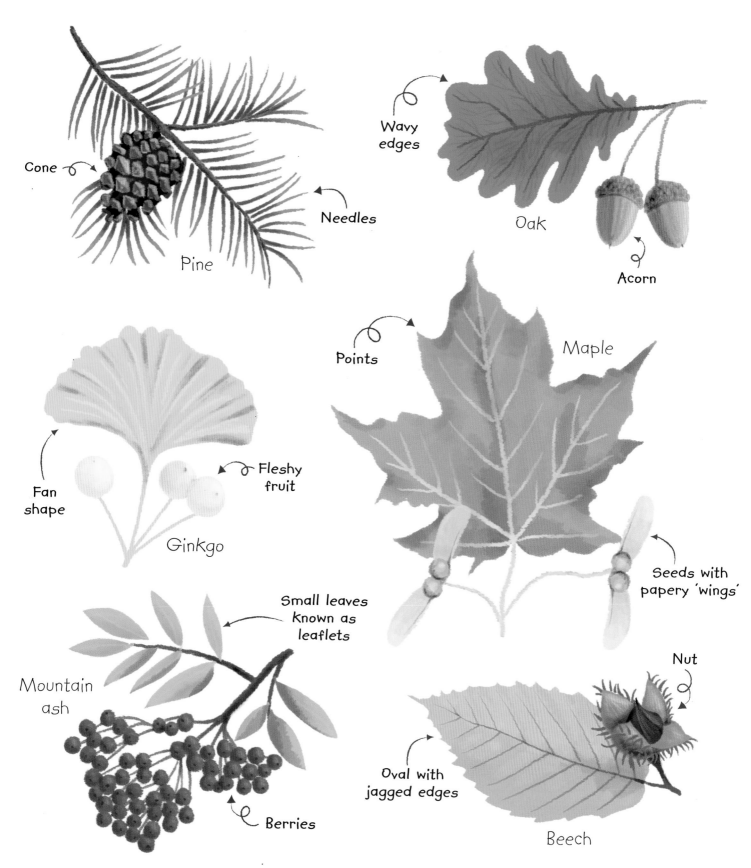

Cone

Needles

Pine

Wavy
edges

Oak

Acorn

Points

Maple

Fan
shape

Fleshy
fruit

Ginkgo

Seeds with
papery 'wings'

Small leaves
known as
leaflets

Nut

Mountain
ash

Oval with
jagged edges

Berries

Beech

Different trees have different types of leaves, fruits and seeds.

All about flowers

Flowers come in many shapes and sizes.
They help plants to make seeds, so new plants can grow.

Dandelion
Stalk

Wild rose
Bush

Magnolia
Tree

Some flowers grow on stalks...   some on bushy plants...   and some on trees.

Daffodil

Cornflower

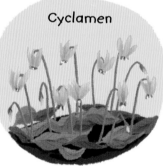
Cyclamen

Snowdrop

Different flowers come out at different times of the year.

Flowers opening

Flowers closing

Some flowers, such as California poppies, turn to face the Sun as it moves across the sky.

Inside a flower is a yellow powder called pollen and a sweet liquid called nectar.

A flower starts as a bud... then opens.

Bees drink nectar, then fly from flower to flower, carrying pollen with them.

Pollen

Fruit

Pollen from a bee tells a flower to start growing fruit.

Parts of the flower fall off as the fruit grows.

Seeds from the fruit end up on the ground. Eventually they grow into new plants.

This is how flowers help a strawberry plant to make seeds.

Making things move

There are many different ways to make things move, but they all use something called FORCE.

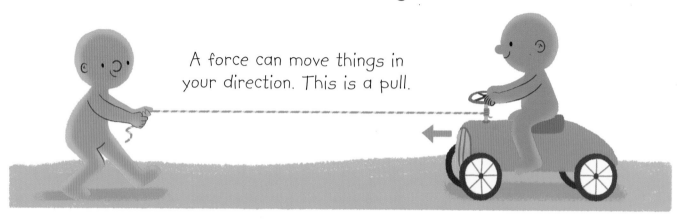

A force can move things in your direction. This is a pull.

A force can also move things away from you. This is a push.

The less force you use to move something, the slower it goes.

If you use MORE force, it will go more quickly.

Some forces work by touching
the thing they're moving...

even if you can't see
this happening.

Some forces work without touching anything. Magnets push and pull
on some things, even if they're not touching them.

An invisible force called gravity pulls things
down to the ground without touching them.

It's gravity that pulls this
toy car down the slope, too.

Experiments to try

A great way to learn more about science is to do some experiments yourself. Ask a grown-up for help before you start.

Beating heart

1. You can feel your heart beat by touching your chest.

2. Jump up and down for a minute.

3. Feel your heart beat again. Is it faster or slower?

Mixing together

1. Drop some liquid food dye into some water.

2. Drop some of the food dye into some oil.

3. Stir each mixture. Can you see a difference?

Sprouting carrot

1. Ask a grown-up to cut the top off a carrot.

2. Put the carrot top on a saucer with some water.

3. Leave in a sunny place and check every day.

Musical bottles

. Take two empty bottles of the same shape and size.

2. Fill one of the bottles with water.

3. Blow over each bottle. Can you hear a difference?

Science experiments don't always go the way you expect. If something surprises you, do the experiment again. If you're still surprised, try to explain what you see.

97

My body

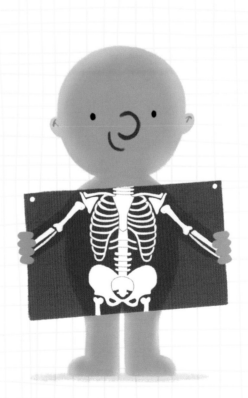

Everybody's body

Everybody is different. People are different shapes and sizes, they have different talents and they enjoy different things.

Some people are old and some are young.

Some people walk and some people rol

Some people are tall and some are short.

Good shot!

Glasses

Stick

Hearing aid

Some people shout and some people make signs.

Guide dog

Some people need help with different parts of their bodies.

But although everyone looks different, they also have some things in common.

Our bodies all need the same three things to keep working.

FOOD...

WATER...

and AIR!

And we're all made of the same stuff - tiny building blocks inside us called cells.

Cells

Different cells do different jobs, but they all work together to keep you alive.

Body parts

Bodies are made from lots of different parts that do different jobs. This is how some of them fit together.

The outside of your body is covered by a layer of skin.

Underneath your skin is a thick layer of stretchy muscles that helps you move.

Under your muscles, there is a hard frame of bones that holds you up. This is your skeleton.

There is a network of blood vessels, too. These are tubes that carry blood to every part of your body.

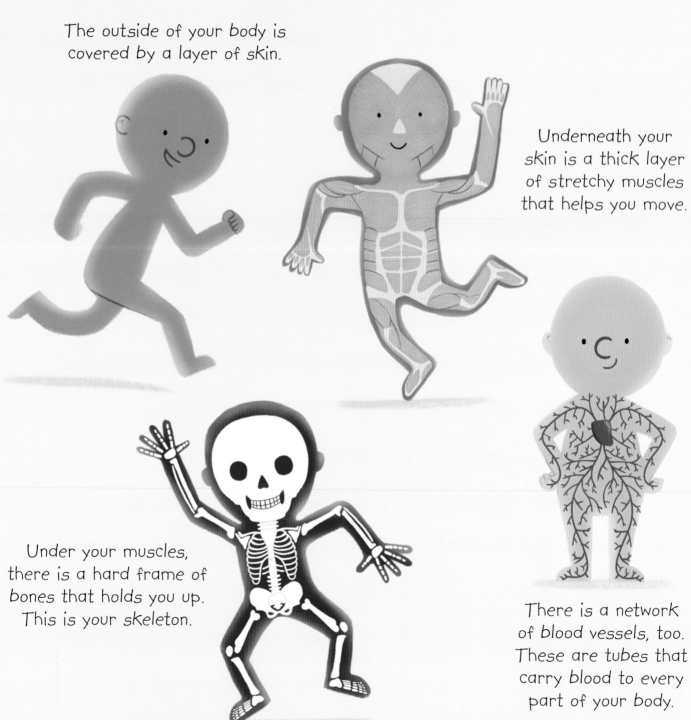

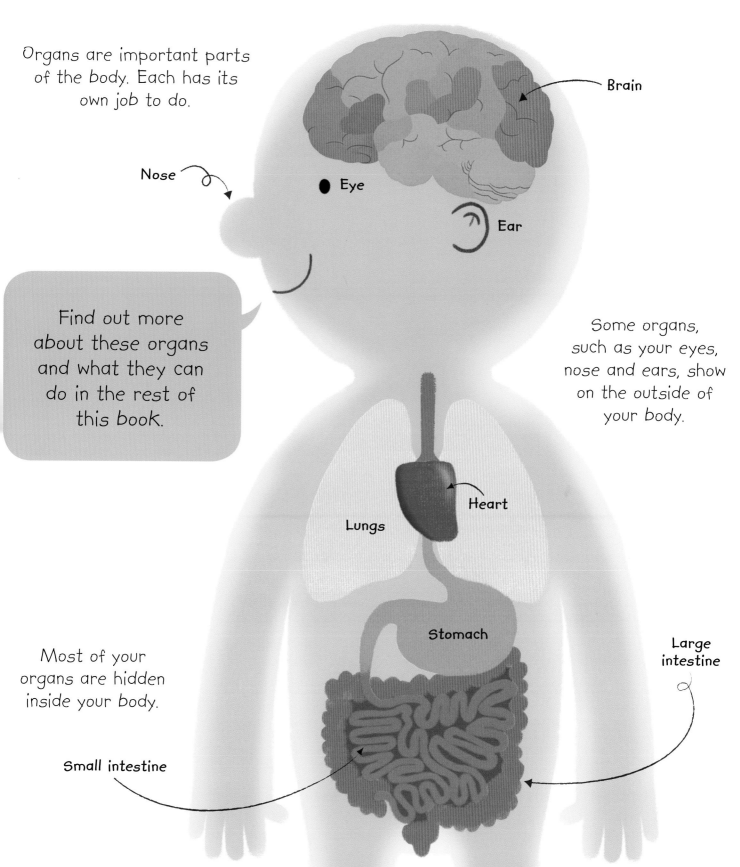

Organs are important parts of the body. Each has its own job to do.

Nose

Eye

Ear

Brain

Find out more about these organs and what they can do in the rest of this book.

Some organs, such as your eyes, nose and ears, show on the outside of your body.

Heart

Lungs

Most of your organs are hidden inside your body.

Stomach

Large intestine

Small intestine

Strong bones

Everyone has hundreds of bones inside their body.
Bones are strong and hard and they fit
together to make a skeleton.

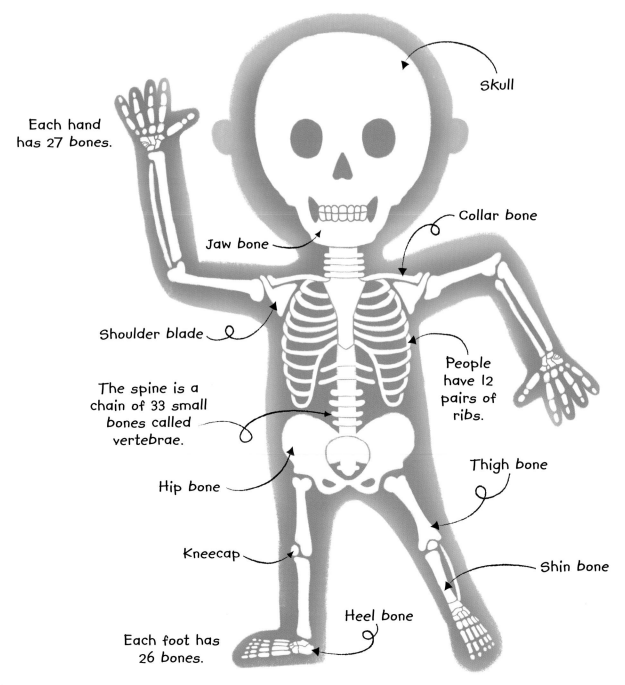

Skull

Each hand
has 27 bones.

Collar bone

Jaw bone

Shoulder blade

People
have 12
pairs of
ribs.

The spine is a
chain of 33 small
bones called
vertebrae.

Thigh bone

Hip bone

Kneecap

Shin bone

Heel bone

Each foot has
26 bones.

People can move their *bodies* at places called joints, where two *bones* join together. Different joints move in different ways.

Bones are strong, but sometimes they can break.

Doctors put cases called casts on them to fix them.

The broken bones grow back together in the cast.

Foods like these help your bones grow strong.

You can also keep your bones healthy by playing outside...

and wearing protective gear for sports.

Muscle power

Muscles are strong and stretchy.
They help people move their bodies.

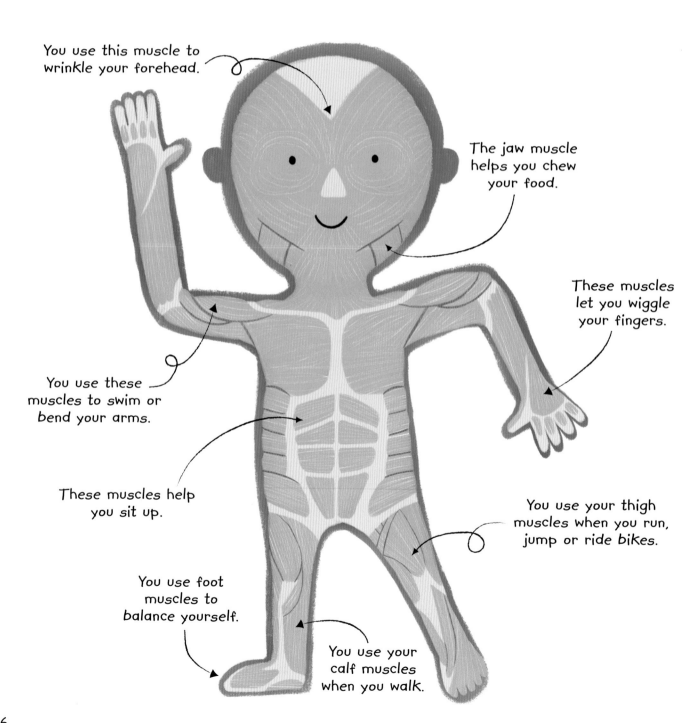

You use this muscle to wrinkle your forehead.

The jaw muscle helps you chew your food.

These muscles let you wiggle your fingers.

You use these muscles to swim or bend your arms.

These muscles help you sit up.

You use your thigh muscles when you run, jump or ride bikes.

You use foot muscles to balance yourself.

You use your calf muscles when you walk.

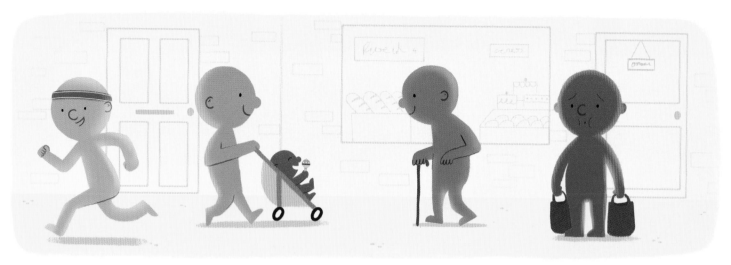

Every time you move your body, you're using muscles.

The more you use your muscles, the stronger they become.

Some muscles work without you thinking about them.
You don't decide to use these muscles, but you can sometimes feel them working.

Sensing the world

There are five main ways that you can sense things, by touching, hearing, seeing, smelling and tasting.

You feel things by touching them.

You hear sounds with your ears.

The busy brain

Inside everyone's head is an organ called the brain. It controls almost everything that you do, using different areas to do different jobs.

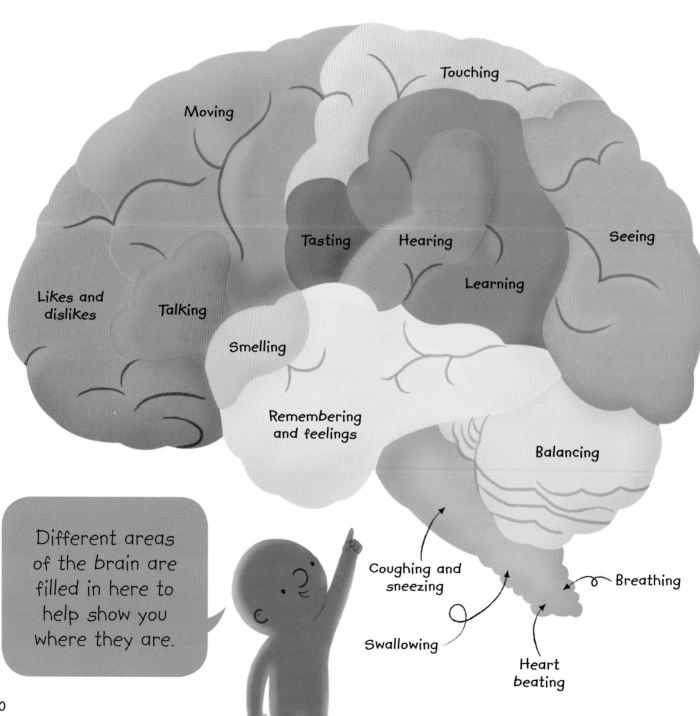

Moving

Touching

Tasting   Hearing   Seeing

Likes and dislikes   Talking   Learning

Smelling

Remembering and feelings

Balancing

Different areas of the brain are filled in here to help show you where they are.

Coughing and sneezing

Breathing

Swallowing

Heart beating

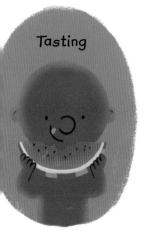
Tasting

Touching

Hearing

Smelling

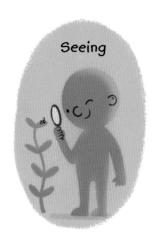
Seeing

Your brain recognizes everything that you sense.

Feelings

Talking

Learning

Balancing

Remembering

Sometimes you know when you're using your brain, such as when you're concentrating or thinking about something.

Coughing and sneezing

Swallowing

Heart beating

Breathing

You also use your brain without realizing it, such as when you blink or breathe. Your brain works all the time to keep you alive.

Eating and drinking

You have to eat food and drink water for your body to work properly. To stay healthy, you need to eat many different types of food.

Broccoli

Cabbage

Avocado

Almonds

Milk

Chicken

Beans

Carrot

Tomato

Spinach

Mushrooms

Yogurt

Fish

Eggs

Everyone needs to be careful not to eat too many sweet, salty or fatty foods.

Berries

Banana

And everyone needs to drink plenty of water, too.

Orange

Snack foods

Chocolate

Pasta

Rice

Butter

Cake

Oats

Bread

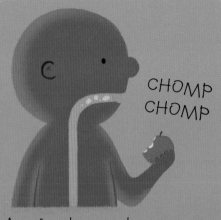

Any food you eat goes on a journey through your body.

Muscles squeeze food pipes to move the food along.

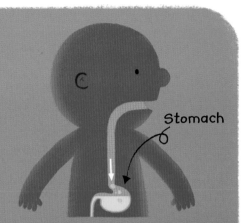

Stomach

The food passes into your stomach.

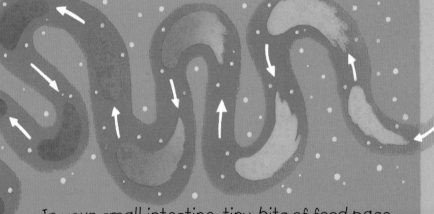

In your small intestine, tiny bits of food pass into your blood and give your body energy to work.

Stomach juices mix with the food, and muscles mush it up.

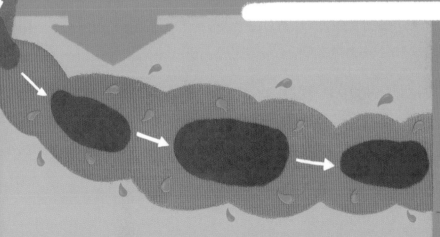

The remaining food moves into your large intestine where water from it passes into your body.

Anything your body doesn't need is pushed out.

Deep breaths

When you breathe air, you take something called oxygen into your body. Everyone needs oxygen to stay alive, so you breathe all the time, even when you're asleep.

People breathe in through their noses and mouths.

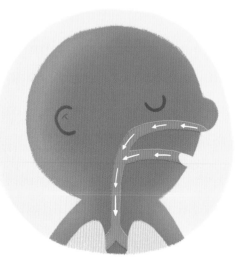

Air travels down a tube known as a windpipe...

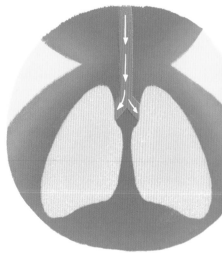

and into a pair of spongy organs called lungs.

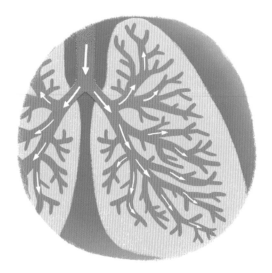

The air travels along smaller and smaller tubes...

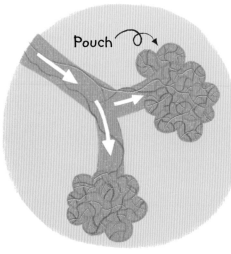

and into tiny pouches...

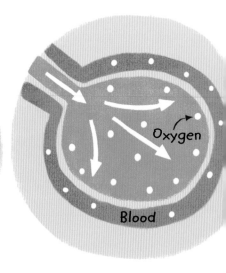

where oxygen from the air passes into the blood.

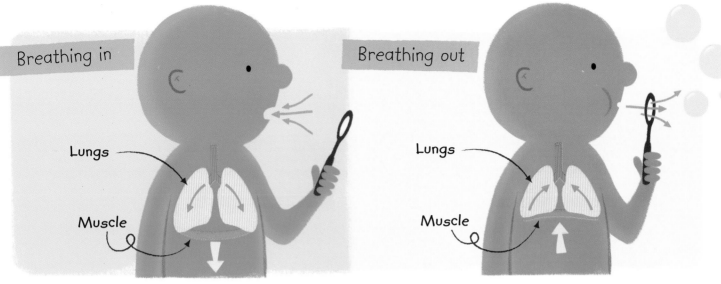

Breathing in

Lungs

Muscle

Breathing out

Lungs

Muscle

A muscle under your lungs helps you breathe by moving up and down.
It pulls down to fill your lungs with air and it springs back up to empty them.

You breathe out leftover air
your body doesn't need.

You cough to clear dirt
from your lungs.

ATCHOO!

You sneeze to clear
dirt from your nose.

When people exercise they can become out of breath.
This is because their bodies are working hard and need more oxygen.

Pumping blood

Your heart is an organ that pumps blood to every part of your body. Your heart never stops pumping and your blood never stops moving – it just travels around and around.

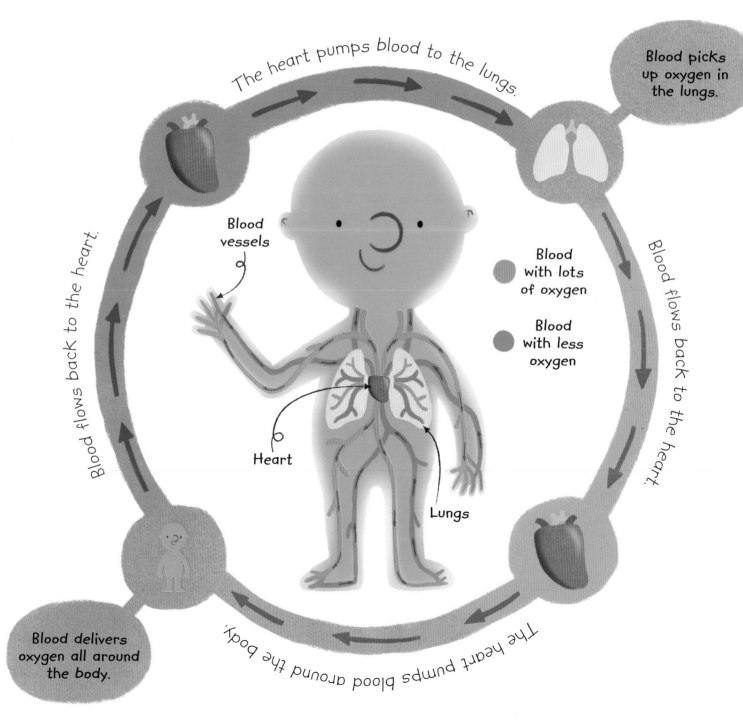

The heart pumps blood to the lungs.

Blood picks up oxygen in the lungs.

Blood flows back to the heart.

Blood flows back to the heart.

Blood vessels

Blood with lots of oxygen

Blood with less oxygen

Heart

Lungs

Blood delivers oxygen all around the body.

The heart pumps blood around the body.

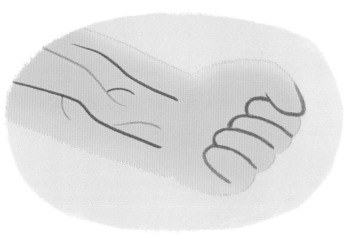

Some blood vessels show through skin. They look like lines.

Doctors can feel your heart pumping blood around your body.

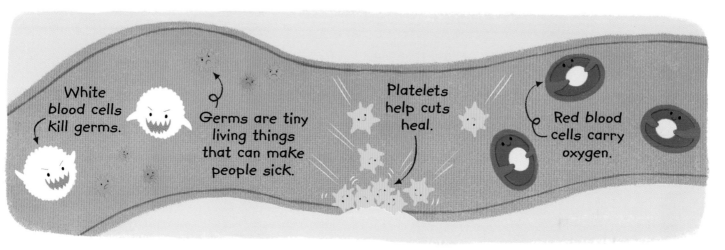

White blood cells kill germs.

Germs are tiny living things that can make people sick.

Platelets help cuts heal.

Red blood cells carry oxygen.

Different things inside blood do different jobs. Some protect the body and some deliver oxygen, food and other things around it.

When a person bleeds, platelets collect near the cut.

This makes the blood sticky, so it dries into a scab.

The scab protects the cut as it heals, then it falls off.

Express yourself

You can use your body to show others what you're thinking and feeling. You can do this by talking, but there are other ways, too.

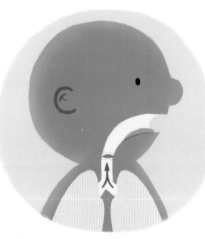

People use air from their lungs when they talk or sing.

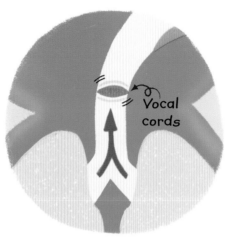

The air wobbles flaps in their throats called vocal cords.

When vocal cords wobble they make sounds come out.

Thank you very much! Thank you!

People use their lips and tongues to turn these sounds into words.

There are many different ways to express yourself.

Higher! HIGHER!

Shouting

Laughing

You don't have to use words.

Psst...

Chatting

Whispering

Gurgling

Crying

Sighing

Making signs

Singing

Cheering

Shaking hands

Raising eyebrows

Frowning

Hugging

You don't even need to make a sound.

Touching

Dancing

Smiling

Folding arms

Waving

119

Sweet dreams

Everybody needs plenty of sleep to keep their bodies and their brains healthy. Most people will spend nearly a third of their lives asleep.

When a person falls asleep, their muscles relax...

they cool down...

Ssssh!

their bodies grow and repair themselves...

their breathing and heart slow down...

and they start to dream.

Sleeping at the end of the day
gives your body a rest...

so you have more energy and feel
fresher when you wake up.

People dream because their brains are
still working when they're asleep.

Scientists think sleep helps the brain
organize itself and remember things.

When people haven't slept
enough they might yawn...

they might start
to feel grumpy...

or they might have dark
circles under their eyes.

Sickness and health

Most of the time, your body works without a problem, but sometimes it doesn't. When this happens you can start to feel unwell.

Coughing

Rash

Earache

Fever

Injury

Feeling very sad

When you feel unwell or hurt yourself, you can visit a doctor. The doctor can find out what's wrong and help you get better.

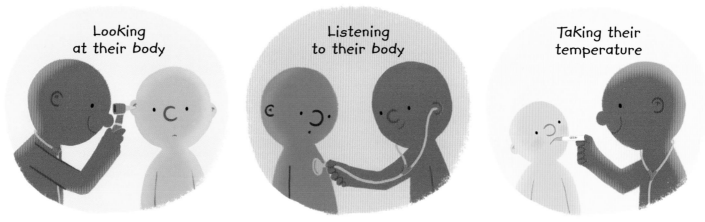

Looking at their body

Listening to their body

Taking their temperature

Sometimes doctors can tell what's wrong
by checking a person's body from the outside.

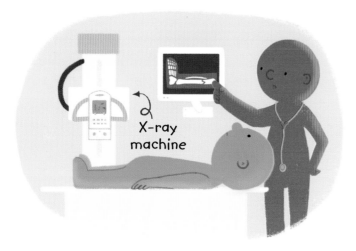

X-ray machine

Sometimes they use machines that
let them *see* inside the body.

Often they can find out what's
wrong just by talking to people.

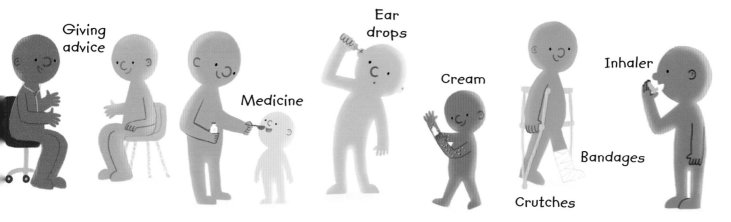

Giving advice

Medicine

Ear drops

Cream

Inhaler

Bandages

Crutches

When doctors know what's wrong, they can help people by
giving them medicines or taking care of them in other ways.

Taking care of your body

When you take care of your body, you're less likely to be unwell. Here are a few things that you can do every day to keep healthy.

Play sports

Ride a bike

Exercising helps your heart and other parts of your body stay healthy.

Run around

Drink plenty of water

Eat different types of food

You'll be stronger and have more energy if you eat and drink sensibly.

Wash yourself

Brush
your teeth

Get enough
sleep

Relax

Staying clean will keep germs away
and stop you from getting sick.

Your body and your brain need
plenty of rest to stay healthy.

Enjoy
hobbies

Learn new
things

Solve
puzzles

Talk about
any problems

Avoid too much
screen time

Your brain needs exercise,
just like your body.

Doing these things will help
you feel happier.

Growing up

Babies grow inside
their mothers.

Newly born babies
grow very quickly.

Later their teeth start
to come through.

Mama!

As children get older,
they learn to talk.

They have more control
of their bodies.

They lose their baby
teeth and grow big ones.

In time, people stop growing
and become grown-ups.

Some grown-ups
have children.

Sometimes their childre
go on to have children.

Their bones become harder and stronger.

Their brains grow and develop quickly.

They learn to crawl and then walk.

They become stronger.

Sometimes they grow in sudden bursts.

They grow more hair and might get pimples.

Their hair might go white or they might get wrinkles.

People may become smaller as they get older.

They might need extra help using their bodies.

Your amazing body

Your body is incredibly hard-working and it's busy every second of your life. It's also quicker and stronger than you might realize and full of other surprises, too.

Your bones are stronger than steel.

Messages from your brain can travel around your body faster than a speeding car.

It can take up to 3 days for the food you eat to pass through your body.

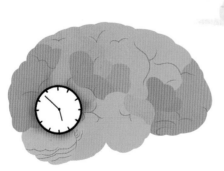

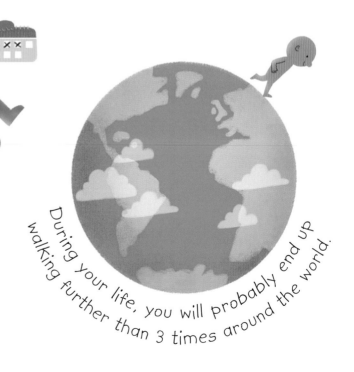

During your life, you will probably end up walking further than 3 times around the world.

A tiny part of your brain works like a clock and keeps track of the time.

Your brain is faster and more powerful than any computer in the world.

Nobody else in the whole world has the same pattern on the tips of their fingers as you.

Most of the dust in your home is made up of tiny pieces of dead skin that have fallen off your body.

You will probably spend more than 22 years of your life asleep.

Most people have enough water in their bodies to fill 190 glasses.

Animals

All sorts of animals

There are millions of different animals living around the world.

Here are some of the animals that live in Africa.

Elephant

Some are very big.

Some are very small.

Dung beetle

Crocodile

Some live on land.

SNAP!

Zebra

Some live in water.

Some can fly.

Eagle

Giraffe

Some can run.

Ostrich

Some are hunters.

Some are hunted.

Some
have fur.

Cheetah

Antelope

Some have
feathers.

Flamingo

Some have
scales.

Python

Growing up

A butterfly has laid
a tiny egg on this leaf.

Out of the egg comes
a caterpillar.

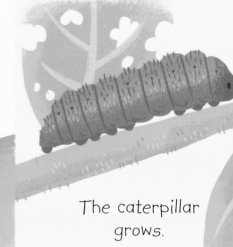

The caterpillar
grows.

Penguin

A mother penguin
has laid an egg.

Parents keep the egg warm
while a chick grows inside.

PEE

A chick hatches
from the egg.

Gorilla

This gorilla is pregnant – a baby
gorilla is growing inside her.

The newborn baby is
carried everywhere.

It gets bigger and
can play on its own

It changes into
a hard chrysalis.

Inside it turns into a
butterfly, then breaks out.

Adult
butterfly

The chick's parents
bring it food.

When it's big enough to swim
on its own, it leaves its parents.

Adult
penguin

Older gorillas teach it
how to be an adult.

After a few years the gorilla
is big, strong and fully grown.

A place to live

Animals need a place to sleep, where they can stay hidden and safe. Many animals build themselves homes to live in and to protect their babies.

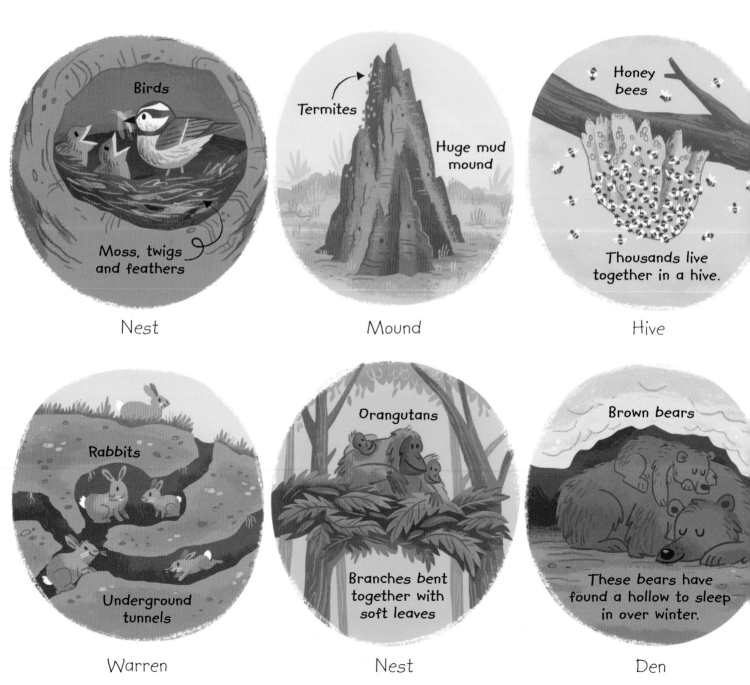

Birds

Moss, twigs and feathers

Nest

Termites

Huge mud mound

Mound

Honey bees

Thousands live together in a hive.

Hive

Rabbits

Underground tunnels

Warren

Orangutans

Branches bent together with soft leaves

Nest

Brown bears

These bears have found a hollow to sleep in over winter.

Den

This rainforest tree is home to lots of different creatures.

Harpy eagles build nests out of sticks.

Sloths sleep on high branches.

A toucan has set up home in the trunk.

Z Z Z Z

Resting jaguar

This anteater has dug a hole to rest in.

Oriole

Oriole birds weave hanging nests.

Tree frogs live on these big leaves.

Sleeping snake

Leaf-cutter ants' nest

Anteater

Finding food

Eating is a big part of an animal's day.
Animals have to find, hunt or catch their own food.

Some animals hunt and eat other animals.
They are called carnivores.

AWOO!

Wolves

Hawks hunt
smaller birds
in mid-air.

This wolf is
stalking a deer.

Grizzly
bear

Salmon

A lynx is looking
for a hare to eat.

This hare is
staying out
of sight.

Duck diving
for fish

Other animals only eat plants.
They are called herbivores.

Red squirrel

Squirrels eat nuts and seeds.

Animals that eat plants and animals are called omnivores.

Deer

Moose grazing on shoots and leaves

Beaver gnawing on tree bark

Vole eating berries

Caterpillar chewing leaves

Wings and feathers

There are thousands of different kinds of birds. They all hatch from eggs, and have feathers, wings and beaks. But they all look and act differently.

Lots of birds live by the sea.

Puffins make nests in the cliffs.

Puffin carrying fish back to its nest

Black-backed gulls

SQUAWK!

This big black-backed gull is snatching food out of a puffin's mouth.

Herring gull

This cormorant is drying out its wings in the sun.

Gannets dive into the water to catch fish.

Woodpeckers tap into trees to find insects to eat.

Swallows sing to each other.

Chickens sit on their eggs to keep them warm.

The bee hummingbird is the smallest bird in the world.

The ostrich is the biggest bird in the world.

Vultures feast on other animals' leftovers.

Flamingos eat pink food. It turns their feathers pink.

Penguins can't fly. They use their wings to swim.

Deadly weapons

Sometimes animals fight to defend themselves,
catch food or prove who is the strongest.
Sharp teeth or claws can help them win the fight.

Antlers

Elk fight to
see who's
toughest.

Jagged teeth
for biting

Piranha

Elephant

Some snakes can
shoot poison through
their fangs.

TSSSSSSSsss

Tusks

Rattlesnake

Underwater town

Lots of sea creatures live in coral reefs.
Reefs are found in warm, shallow water,
and are full of light and life.

Sponge

Cuttlefish

Anemone

Corals look like plants,
but they're animals. Lots of
corals make up a reef. They
give fish safe places to live.

Turtle

Some corals
are hard.

Some corals
are soft.

Cardinalfish

Triggerfish

This seahorse blends in with the coral.

Reef shark

Snapper

Parrotfish

Clownfish

Spiky sea urchin

Sometimes different animals team up. They can live better together than on their own.

Clownfish keep this anemone clean.

The anemone gives clownfish a safe home.

Starfish

Anemones and sponges are animals too.

Eel

Bugs and slugs

There are more creepy crawlies in the world than any other type of animal. They're small, but there are millions of them.

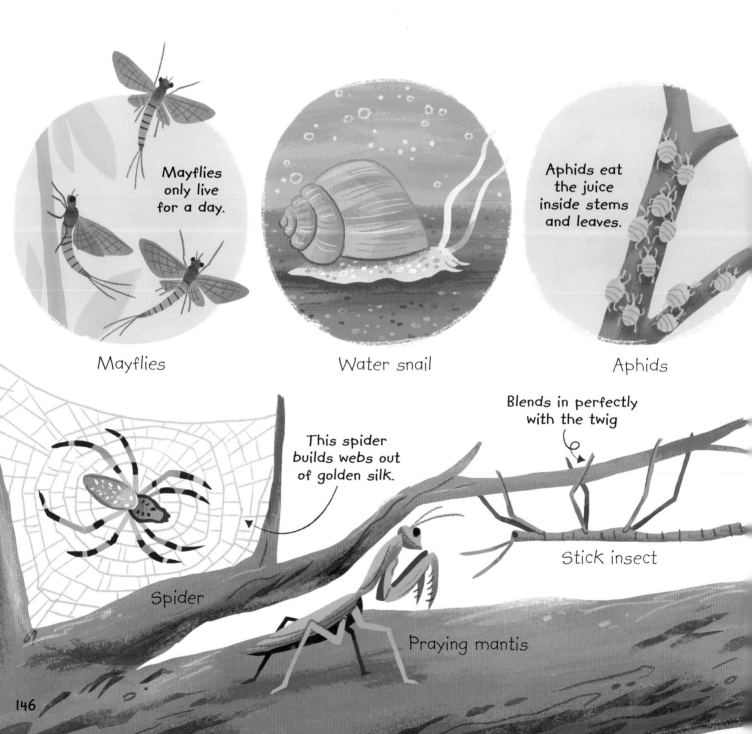

Mayflies only live for a day.

Mayflies

Water snail

Aphids eat the juice inside stems and leaves.

Aphids

This spider builds webs out of golden silk.

Spider

Praying mantis

Blends in perfectly with the twig

Stick insect

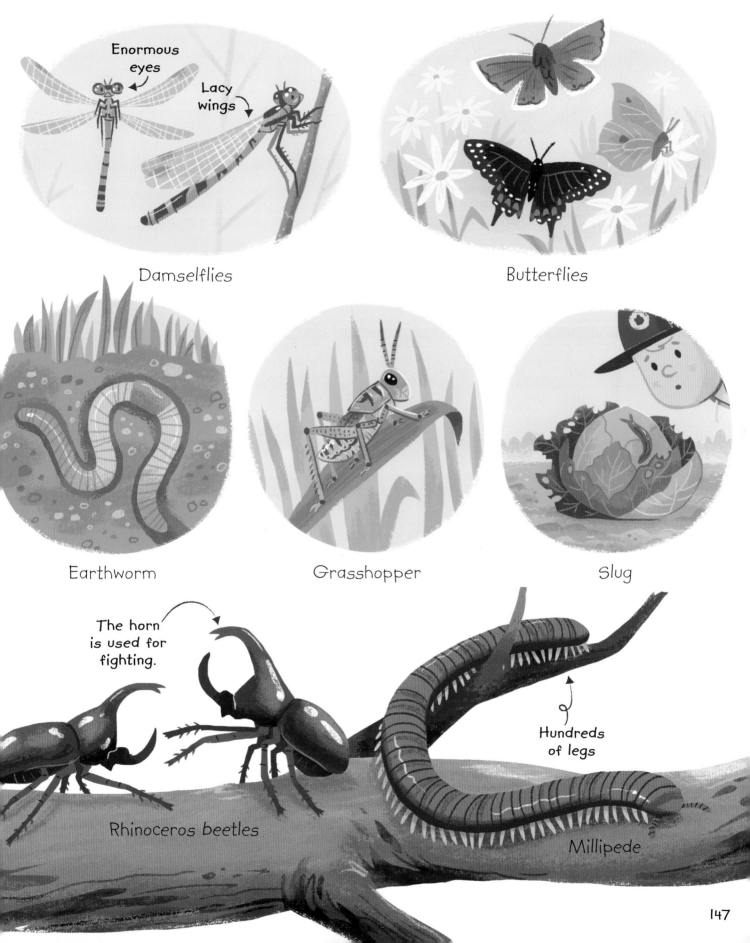

Damselflies

Butterflies

Earthworm

Grasshopper

Slug

The horn is used for fighting.

Rhinoceros beetles

Hundreds of legs

Millipede

Hot and cold

Some animals live in places where
it's baking hot or freezing cold.

Camels store fat in their
humps. They turn it into energy
when they can't find food.

This gazelle
has found some
grass to eat.

Scorpion

Dung beetles

Lizards

This viper has horns
that might stop sand
from getting in its eyes.

Sand foxes

This is a hot, dry desert. There's not much water and hardly any plants.
Most of the animals here are pale, to blend in with the sand.

This is the frozen Arctic. Not much can live here and not much grows.
Everything is white with snow and ice. Most of the animals are white too, to blend in.

Patterns

Lots of animals are bright and beautiful, with spotted fur, striped skin or flashy feathers, to help them hide or stand out.

Panther chameleon

Chameleons can turn their skin green to blend in with leaves.

Moon jellyfish

This jellyfish is see-through, to disguise it in the ocean.

Leopards are the same shade as the grass they skulk in.

Fancy patterns stand out from the crowd.
They say, "Look at me!"

A peacock's tail helps him impress females.

Birds of paradise

Peacock

Bright cheeks

Chameleons completely change how they look, to show off.

Mandrill

Bright stripes or spots can mean,
"Don't eat me - I'm dangerous!"

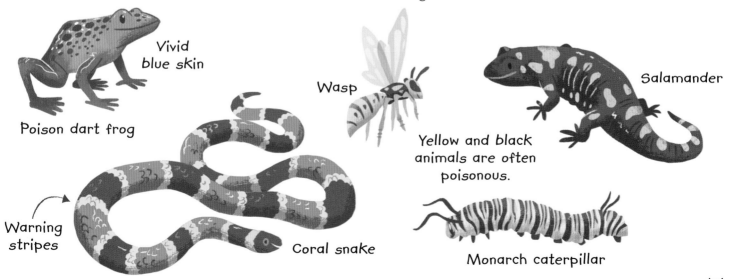

Vivid blue skin

Poison dart frog

Wasp

Salamander

Yellow and black animals are often poisonous.

Warning stripes

Coral snake

Monarch caterpillar

Sending messages

Animals use sounds and smells to send messages to each other – sometimes they're friendly and sometimes they're fearsome.

Dolphins whistle and click to send each other messages.

CLICK
CLICK

WHISTLE

Birds sing to attract mates to have babies with.

CHIRP
CHIRP

Chimpanzees

These chimps are hugging to make friends.

Hippopotamus

Hippos spread smelly dung around to keep others away.

The deer with the loudest roar takes charge.

Praying mantises spread their legs to look bigger and scare off other animals.

Skunks spray a smelly liquid to tell attackers not to come closer.

Pufferfish puff out their stomachs to warn bigger fish they'd be hard to eat.

153

In the dark

Some animals spend most of their lives in the dark, some under the sea, some only coming out at night.

Lanternfish

These fish make their own light.

Angler fish

Frilled shark

Vampire squid

Deep sea creatures have soft bendy bones.

Blobfish

Light from the sun doesn't reach the deepest parts of the ocean.
The deeper you go, the harder it is to live.

Some animals sleep during the day and come out when the sun sets and it gets dark.

Bats

Fireflies

Moths

Barn owl chicks

Barn owl

TWIT TWOO!

Sleeping bat

Animals that come out at night are called nocturnal animals.

Foxes

Wood mouse

Hedgehog

CROAK
Toad catching insects

Otter

Night animals have good noses and ears
so they can find their way around in the dark.

Animal journeys

Animals are always on the move, but some go on amazingly long journeys. They travel across the planet each year to find food, sunshine, or to lay their eggs.

Green turtles

Turtles swim across oceans back to where they were hatched, to lay their own eggs.

Red crabs all hatch at once, and travel together to the sea.

Red crabs

African elephants

Elephants walk miles and miles every day to find enough food to fill them up.

Long animal journeys are called migrations.

Geese

When it gets cold, geese and monarch butterflies fly south in huge flocks, to find warmth and food.

Monarch butterflies

Every year millions of wildebeest trek across Africa, looking for green grass.

Wildebeest

Humpback whale

Huge humpback whales travel far and wide, swimming thousands of miles every year.

157

Where in the world?

Seal

Eagle

Wolf

North America

Polar bear

Coyote

Alligator

Killer whale

Gorilla

Pacific Ocean

Snake

Jaguar

Jellyfish

Butterfly

Atlantic Ocean

South America

This is a map of the world, showing where different animals come from.

Toucan

Chameleon

Squid

Llama

Penguin

Reindeer

Beluga whale

Walrus

Otter

Camel

Panda

Macaque

Europe

Asia

Scorpion

Dung beetle

Parakeet

Turtle

Africa

Tiger

Fish

African elephant

Orangutan

Indian Ocean

Coral

Spider

Kangaroo

Great white shark

Giraffe

Australasia

Kiwi

Antarctica

159

Record breakers

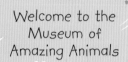
Loudest

Howler monkeys' calls can be heard clearly for 5km (3 miles).

How loud can you call?

Oooh ooh!

180,000kg (400,000lbs)

How heavy are you?

25kg (55lb) That's the same as a wolf.

Biggest
Blue whale

Albatross birds have a wingspan of 3m (10ft)

Fastest in the sea

How fast can you run?

Sailfish Swims at 110kph (68mph)

Flamingos can stand on one leg for hours at a time.

Strongest
Dung beetles can shift over a thousand times their own weight.
Oof!
How strong are you?
Smallest
The world's tiniest frog could sit on the tip of your finger.
Smelliest
Skunk
Stinkbird
Bombardier beetle
Which animal smells worst?
Yuck!
Sniff here
A whale's heart alone weighs the same as a cow!
30m long (100ft)
That whale is bigger than a dinosaur!
Fastest on land
Cheetah
Runs at 120kph (75mph)
Peregrine falcon
Dives at 390kph (240mph)
Fastest in the sky

Dinosaurs

In the time of the dinosaurs

Long, long ago, before there were any people, planet Earth was home to creatures known as dinosaurs.

'Dinosaur' means 'terrible lizard'.
Some dinosaurs were big and frightening,
but others were surprisingly small.

Apatosaurus

Camarasaurus

Stokesosaurus

Allosaurus

Gargoyleosaurus

Some dinosaurs had scaly skin.
Others, like these, had feathers.

Othnielosaurus

Ornitholestes

Dinosaurs shared their world with other animals that weren't dinosaurs.

This flying Scaphognathus isn't a dinosaur.

Brachiosaurus

Ceratosaurus

Goniopholis...

...isn't a dinosaur.

Volaticotherium

These small, furry creatures aren't dinosaurs.

Fruitafossor

Big and small

Dinosaurs were the largest animals that have ever walked on land. Nobody knows which type was the very biggest, because people keep finding bigger bones.

Some dinosaurs were rather small. The smallest we know of were around the size of a duck.

Human being

Microraptor

Minmi

Citipati

Protoceratops

Microceratus

Ankylosaurus

Compsognathus

This tail alone was the same length as a python.

These legs were twice the height of an adult human.

These horns were as long as a human arm.

Triceratops

Tyrannosaurus rex

This dinosaur's head was almost as big as a human being.

This dinosaur lived in water.

Spinosaurus

This massive dinosaur was heavier than twenty elephants put together.

Its neck was at least three times longer than a giraffe's neck.

Diplodocus

Stegosaurus

167

Where did dinosaurs come from?

Dinosaurs weren't the first animals that lived on the Earth. Before them, came crawling animals – and even before them, there were swimming animals in the sea.

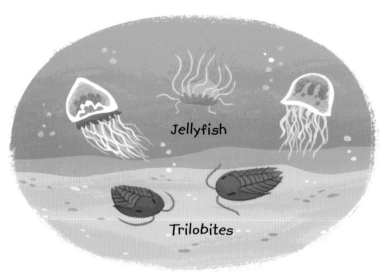

The very first animals swam or floated under water. They had no arms or legs.

Fish with flippers were the first creatures to crawl out of the water.

Some of the first animals that lived on land were scaly creatures a little like dinosaurs. Their legs stuck out on either side, and they crawled with their bellies close to the ground.

The very first dinosaurs appeared – along with lots of other animals – many, many years later. These dinosaurs walked on two legs, that stuck straight down under their bodies.

Mussaurus

Riojasaurus

Staurikosaurus

Herrerasaurus

Exaeretodon
(not a dinosaur)

Eoraptor

Ischigualastia
(not a dinosaur)

Inside a dinosaur

No one really knows what any dinosaur looked like on the outside. But we know a lot about their bones, and some other inside parts, too.

The bones in a skeleton reveal a lot about what shape a dinosaur was. The blue outline shows the shape of an Argentinosaurus – an enormous plant-eating dinosaur.

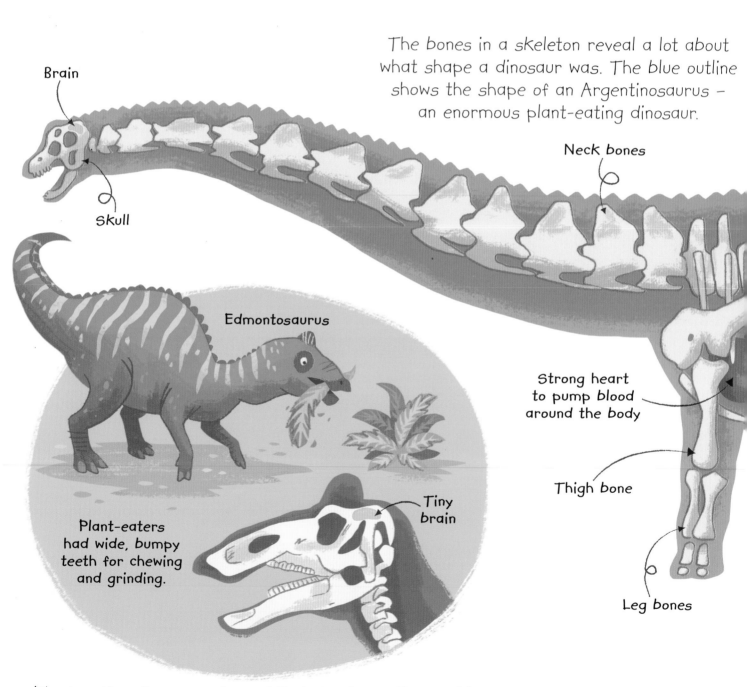

Brain

Skull

Neck bones

Edmontosaurus

Strong heart to pump blood around the body

Thigh bone

Tiny brain

Plant-eaters had wide, bumpy teeth for chewing and grinding.

Leg bones

Plant-eating dinosaurs chewed their food very thoroughly.

Most meat-eaters were smaller than plant-eaters. But they had *big brains* for their size.

Troodon

Big brain

Meat eaters had sharp teeth for biting and tearing flesh.

Meat-eating dinosaurs gulped down their food.

Back bones

Muscles around the tail bones to make it swish

Food sat in their guts for days and days.

Big dinosaurs ate so much they often swallowed stones and branches by accident.

Growing up

All dinosaurs, big and small, hatched from eggs.
Even the largest dinosaurs laid eggs that were
no bigger than a football.

A mother Citipati has just
laid a clutch of eggs.

The father sits on the nest
to keep the eggs warm.

Inside each egg, a tiny
baby Citipati grows.

After a few weeks, the
eggs are ready to hatch.

The babies peck their
way out from inside.

The parents bring food
for the children.

Some dinosaurs grew up in small groups called packs,
or in enormous herds. Others lived on their own.

A lone hunter

Maiasaurus
graze together
in large herds.

Ornithomimus
roam in a pack.

These dinosaurs are a
year old. They're nearly
adult-sized already.

Some dinosaurs leave their
eggs to hatch on their own.

These Maiasaurus babies
have just hatched.

Up in the air

While dinosaurs roamed on land, flying creatures
known as pterosaurs soared through the sky.

Here are some pterosaurs
that lived by the sea.

Pterodactylus

Gnathosaurus

Scaphognathus

Rhamphorhynchus

Aerodactylus

Anurognathus

From end to end, these wings spread the length of a bus.

Bright crest

Hatzegopteryx

Pterosaurs were the biggest flying creatures that have ever existed.

Archaeopteryx

Confuciusornis

Quetzalcoatlus

Standing up, a Quetzalcoatlus was as tall as a giraffe.

Pterosaurs weren't the only animals with wings. Some dinosaurs had wings they used for gliding or flying.

Under the sea

In the time of the dinosaurs, massive creatures with big teeth prowled the oceans.

Plesiosaurus

Ichthyosaurus

Excalibosaurus

Macroplata

Rhomaleosaurus

Stenopterygius

Callipterus

Shark

Coelacanth

Mosasaurus

Giant squid

Platecarpus

Around the time most dinosaurs died out, the sea was home to all sorts of fierce creatures with sharp teeth or long tentacles.

Tylosaurus

Elasmosaurus

Ammonites

What happened to the dinosaurs?

Many millions of years ago, a huge disaster killed off all kinds of animals, including dinosaurs. Scientists are still trying to learn exactly how it happened.

It all began when an enormous rock from space came crashing into planet Earth...

...the rock made a hole in a place called Yucatan, on the east coast of Mexico.

Alamosaurus

Tyrannosaurus

Edmontosaurus

Triceratops

Tylosaurus

The crashing rock set off many earthquakes and tsunamis.

Huge clouds of dust filled the sky.

The dust spread out and covered the Earth.

It grew cold and dark, and many plants died out...

...so all the plant-eating dinosaurs died out, too.

And, in time, so did the meat-eaters.

But a few small animals survived. These included furry mammals, and feathered dinosaurs – now called birds.

Bones and fossils

Dinosaur hunters are called paleontologists.
They dig into the ground to find the remains
of long-dead dinosaurs.

Millions of years ago...

A dinosaur dies and its
body is covered in mud.

Its body rots away,
leaving only a skeleton.

Hundreds of years later, it's
buried under layers of rock.

When it rains, water
trickles into the bones.

Chemicals in the water
react with the bones...

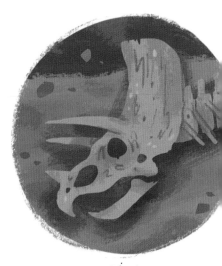

...and slowly turn
them into fossils.

Millions of years later...

Rain and wind wear away the rocks and the fossils.

A few fossils end up near the surface of the soil...

...where a fossil hunter can find them.

Paleontologists dig up the fossils very carefully.

Then they scrape all the dirt off.

Often, many fossil bones are missing.

Paleontologists make new bones to fill in any missing pieces.

Paleontologists have to work out how all the bones fit together.

The changing world of dinosaurs

Dinosaurs didn't all live at the same time. Over the years, they appeared in many different shapes and sizes, too.

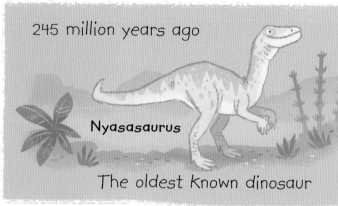

245 million years ago

Nyasasaurus

The oldest known dinosaur

110 million years ago

Aquilops

The first dinosaurs with horns

150 million years ag[o]

Archaeopteryx

The oldest known birds

90 million years ago

Argentinosaurus

The biggest known dinosaurs

Timeline of animals

The first ever animals

The first fish

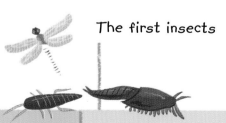

The first insects

The first reptiles

500 million years ago

400 million years ago

300 milli[on] years ag[o]

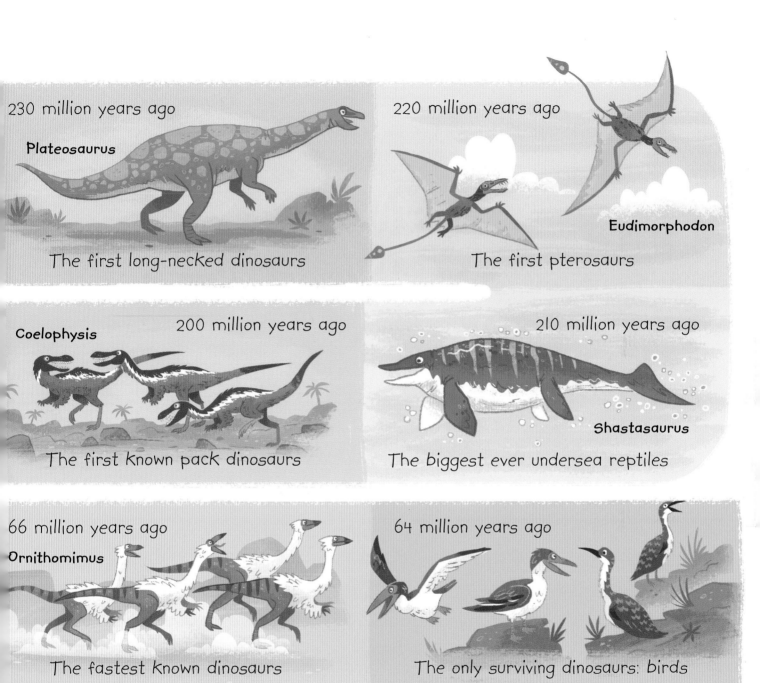

230 million years ago

Plateosaurus

The first long-necked dinosaurs

220 million years ago

Eudimorphodon

The first pterosaurs

Coelophysis

200 million years ago

The first known pack dinosaurs

210 million years ago

Shastasaurus

The biggest ever undersea reptiles

66 million years ago

Ornithomimus

The fastest known dinosaurs

64 million years ago

The only surviving dinosaurs: birds

The first dinosaurs

200 million years ago

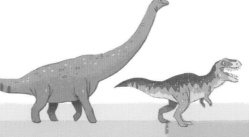

100 million years ago

A great disaster kills off many animals

The first people

Now

Long ago

The Stone Age

Thousands of years ago, people didn't live in houses or grow food on farms. They moved from place to place, looking for food in the wild.

Hunting

Chopping wood

Stone axes

Digging for roots

Picking nuts and berries

Tent covered with animal skin

Drying animal skins

Drying meat

Clothes made from animal skin

Fur cloak

Antler harpoon

Cooking on a fire

Fishing

Tree trunk canoe

186

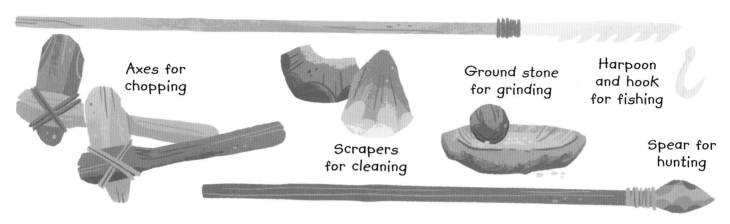

Axes for chopping

Scrapers for cleaning

Ground stone for grinding

Harpoon and hook for fishing

Spear for hunting

This time is called the Stone Age because people made tools from stones, and sometimes deer antlers, bone and wood too.

After a while, some Stone-Age people found out how to grow their own food. They started to build houses and settle in one place.

Sickle for cutting crops

Ornaments

Cooking pot

Tools and weapons

Later still, people learned to make strong, sharp tools from a metal called bronze and ornaments from gold. This time is called the Bronze Age.

The Pharaoh's land

People now known as the Ancient Egyptians lived along the River Nile in North Africa. Here they built magnificent temples and tombs called pyramids.

Pyramid

Temple

Fishermen

Trader's ship

Sphinx statues guard the temple

It's scorching today.

Papyrus boat

School

Ferry across the Nile

I wish girls could go to school.

Papyrus plants

Market

Figs   Dates

Radishes and lettuce

Wheat

Shaduf for lifting water

Mud bricks

This is a canal. It brings river water inland.

Most of Ancient Egypt was a dusty desert, but the River Nile flowed through the whole country, carrying boats and bringing water to grow food.

Priest

Gifts for the pharaoh

Musicians

Pharaoh

Ostrich feather fan

Throne

Ancient Egypt was ruled by a powerful King called a pharaoh.

Spells written in a picture writing called hieroglyphics

Stone headrest to sleep on (instead of a pillow)

Perfumes

Golden furniture

Clothes

Solid gold coffin

Jewels

Games

Preserved food

The Ancient Egyptians believed in a life after death, so they buried their pharaohs with things for them to use after they died.

The Iron Age

A time Known as the Iron Age began in Europe, when people learned to make things from a strong metal called iron.

People looked for rocks called iron ore.

They heated iron ore in a very hot oven to make iron.

The iron could be hammered into any shape.

Iron-Age people lived and worked together in groups called tribes.

Tribes built tall fences and steep banks around their homes to Keep out enemies.

Every tribe had a chief who made decisions and led them into battle.

Priests called druids performed religious ceremonies.

Warriors were trained to use weapons to defend the tribe.

A bard told stories and sang songs about the tribe's great leaders.

Most Iron-Age people worked as farmers.

Craftworkers made things from iron, wood and clay.

Roving Romans

The Romans were people from the city of Rome in Italy. Their army conquered vast amounts of land where they built new cities, and roads linking them together.

Crested helmet

Sword

Scabbard
(sword holder)

Dagger

Shield

Breastplate

These things are a Roman soldier's battle gear.

Tunic

Javelin
for throwing

Protective apron

Sandals

This is an aqueduct. It carries fresh water into the city.

At the heart of every Roman city was a public square known as a forum. People would meet there, shop and listen to speeches.

Tang China

At this time, China was ruled by a family of emperors called the Tang. Under the Tang, the country became peaceful and rich.

Palace

Pagoda

Over a million people lived in the Tang city of Chang'an. There were many majestic palaces and towers called pagodas inside the city walls.

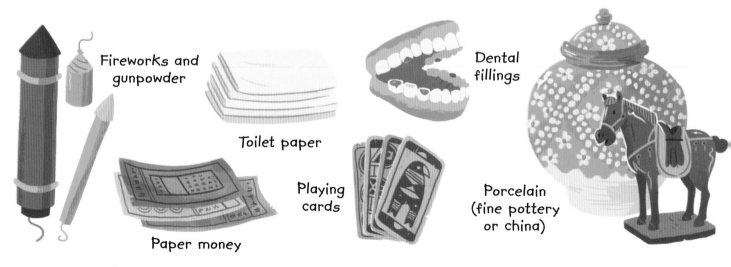

Fireworks and gunpowder

Toilet paper

Paper money

Playing cards

Dental fillings

Porcelain (fine pottery or china)

Lots of inventions made by people from the Tang dynasty are still used today.

Tang emperors set a difficult exam to find the cleverest people to help them run the country. The exam covered lots of subjects.

Archery

Law

Mathematics

Music

Fighting

Poetry

Only one out of every hundred people passed the test.

Mighty Maya

The Maya were people who lived in Central America. They cleared large areas of jungle to build several big cities, each with its own King.

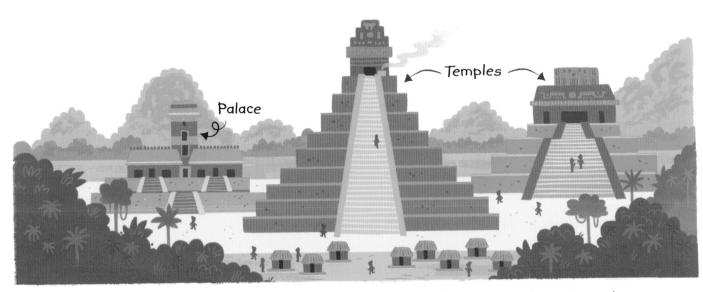

Every Maya city had a palace, where the King lived, and stone temples, where some Kings were buried and astronomers studied the stars.

Important cities also had a ball court for a game called *Pok a Tok*. The Maya didn't just play this game for fun, it was also part of their religion.

| Sky | Cloud | Fire | Mountain | Sun | Snake |

The Maya invented a way of writing using symbols, called glyphs, which stood for different words or sounds.

Corn

Avocados

Tomatoes

Red and black beans

Peppers

Squash

Most ordinary Maya worked as farmers, growing food to feed people in the city.

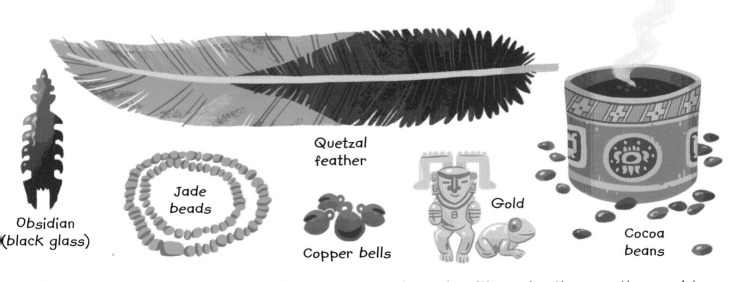

Obsidian (black glass)

Jade beads

Quetzal feather

Copper bells

Gold

Cocoa beans

The Maya didn't have money. They exchanged goods with each other, or they paid with feathers, cocoa or objects made from valuable materials such as gold.

Sailors and raiders

People called Vikings lived in Northern Europe.
They were famous for being fierce warriors,
but they were also farmers, craftworkers
and excellent sailors.

When good farming land ran out,
the Vikings looked for new opportunities.

Some made their living away
from farms, learning new crafts.

Some went to live in other parts of
Europe and even reached North America.

Meanwhile, Viking traders roamed
as far away as Baghdad in Iraq.

Before Vikings settled in new places, they often attacked or raided local towns and villages, taking people prisoner and stealing their treasure.

199

Castle town

Hundreds of years ago, people all over Europe were fighting wars with each other. To keep safe, kings and lords built strong castles and, later on, tall walls around towns.

Guard

Lord and lady

No one will be able to climb my new town walls.

Castle

Tailor

Carpenter

Inn

Warmest wool cloth for winter!

That'll teach you not to sell stale fish!

Pillory

Blacksmith

Cloth merchant

Well

Lute

Acrobats

Squire (trainee Knight)

Farm animals for sale

Troubador (wandering musician)

Knights

201

City of mud

Adventurous traders risked their lives to reach Timbuktu in West Africa. The city became famous for its universities, libraries and great wealth.

Timbuktu grew up where the sandy Sahara desert met the River Niger.

Gold-seeking traders rested here after dangerous desert journeys.

The traders set up a market where they swapped goods and slaves with each other.

The traders grew rich, building grand houses and city walls from mud bricks.

In Timbuktu's busy markets, people could buy salt from the north, gold from the south and books from the east.

The traders spread the Muslim faith and brought scholars with them who set up one of the world's first universities in Timbuktu.

Buzzing London

London in England was an exciting, crowded city. It grew bigger and bigger as people moved from the country, hoping to make their fortune.

During especially cold winters, the River Thames froze solid. Frost fairs were held on the ice, where people would skate, set up stalls and play games.

Ships brought goods from all over the world to London's busy port.

Some people were very poor. They were forced to steal and beg to make a living.

Famous writers, such as William Shakespeare, wrote plays that were performed in playhouses in front of a crowd that could be loud and rowdy.

Old Japan

Edo (the old name for Tokyo) in Japan was the largest city in the world. This time in Japanese history is known as the Edo period.

During the Edo period, Japan had emperors, but they didn't have any power. Instead, leaders called shoguns ruled the country from a castle in Edo.

Edo people loved nature. They grew beautiful gardens and arranged flowers.

They drank tea together to relax, as part of a ceremony with strict rules.

Sword

Side
sword

Shoulder
guard

Helmet

Mask

Chest guard

Arm
guard

Leg guard

Skirt

Tabi (toe socks)

Soldiers known as samurai wore fierce-looking clothes for fighting.
This was mostly for show, because the Edo period was so peaceful.

In their free time, people watched shows called kabuki plays.
Actors wore elaborate make-up and danced to music.

The Gold Rush

The Gold Rush was a time when people
from all over the world hurried to California
in North America, hoping to find gold.

The first people in California
were Native Americans.

Thousands of years later,
Europeans arrived.

Later still, two men
found gold in the area.

The news spread all
around the world.

You'll be safe if you follow me.

Thousands of people set off to find gold, but there
were no maps, so trail guides showed the way.

At first, miners found gold in river water.

Then they started to dig for it underground.

The miners forced the Native Americans to leave.

Sometimes there were fights over land.

Only a few miners found their fortune in the gold mines, but local traders grew very rich.

After a while, gold became harder to find.

Many miners went home empty handed.

Some chose to stay and farm the land.

Factory town

Lots of people in Britain worked in factories.
They burned coal to power new steam engines which
could drive ships, trains and machines.

How do we know about long ago?

You can learn about life in the past by visiting museums and old buildings. Here you can find treasures that people have saved from long ago.

Edo costume
(300 years ago)

Native American costume
(170 years ago)

Painting of London
(400 years ago)

Knight costume
(800 years ago)

Some art shows how people and places used to look long ago.

Tang pottery
(1,400 years ago)

Roman statue
(2,000 years ago)

Fire truck
(130 years ago)

Viking ship
(1,000 years ago)

People long ago didn't have cars.

They walked or they used horses or boats to get around.

Some objects from long ago are found buried underground.

Stone-Age axes
(10,000 years ago)

Iron-Age sword
(2,500 years ago)

Ancient Egyptian mummy
(3,500 years ago)

Books from Timbuktu
(600 years ago)

A few people long ago wrote things down about their lives and beliefs.

Maya carving
(1,200 years ago)

People who dig up old objects to learn about the past are called archaeologists.

Where and when?

These pages haven't only taken you on a journey through time, they've also taken you on a trip around the world. Look back through the pages to see who lived where – as well as when.

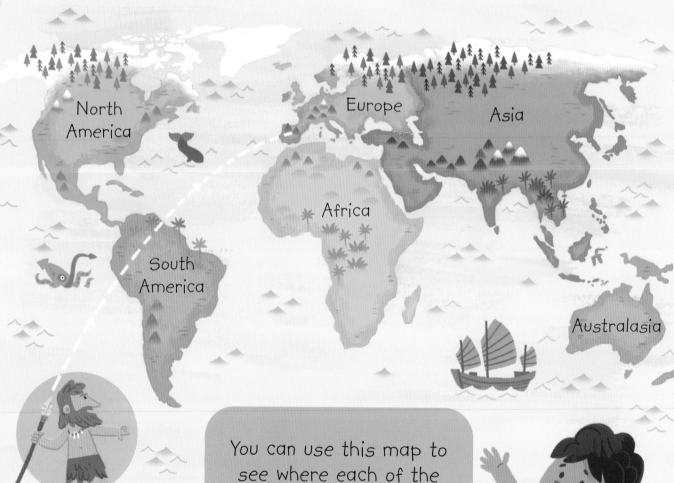

North America

Europe

Asia

Africa

South America

Australasia

Stone-Age hunter
Europe
10,000 years ago

You can use this map to see where each of the characters on the next page lived.

Ancient Egyptian musician
Africa
3,500 years ago

Iron-Age farmer
Europe
2,500 years ago

Roman soldier
Europe
2,000 years ago

Tang poet
Asia
1,400 years ago

Maya ball player
North America
1,200 years ago

Viking warrior
Europe
1,000 years ago

Castle knight
Europe
800 years ago

Timbuktu trader
Africa
600 years ago

London lady
Europe
400 years ago

Edo woman
Asia
300 years ago

Gold Rush miner
North America
170 years ago

Factory worker
Europe
130 years ago

Index

I

J

K

L

M

T

Usborne Quicklinks

The internet is a great place for discovering more about the topics in this book.
For links to carefully selected websites for young children, go to
usborne.com/Quicklinks and type in the title of this book.

You'll find links to websites where you can...

...visit the North Pole and see how animals keep warm
...see where an astronaut sleeps on the International Space Station
...watch a video about forces that make things move
...take a peek at your brain and other organs
...find out about the biggest animal on Earth, the blue whale

...and much, much more.

Notes for grown-ups

Please read the internet safety guidelines at Usborne Quicklinks with your child. Children should be supervised online. The websites are regularly reviewed and the links at Usborne Quicklinks are updated. However, Usborne Publishing is not responsible and does not accept liability for the content or availability of any website other than its own.

Expert advisors: Penny Coltman, Dr. Owen Lewis, Dr. Anne Millard,
Dr. Darren Naish, Zoë Simmons, John & Margaret Rostron, Dr. Roger Trend

Managing designer: Nicola Butler

Edited by: Ruth Brocklehurst, Jane Chisholm & Abigail Wheatley

The publishers are grateful to the following for permission to reproduce material:
Page 44: © Stockbyte/Getty Images (the Moon); Page 60: © SOHO/ESA/NASA/Science Photo Library (the Sun); Page 62: © NASA, ESA, and the Hubble Heritage Team (STScI/AURA) (the Tarantula Nebula); Page 67: © NASA, ESA, G. Illingworth, D. Magee, and P. Oesch (University of California, Santa Cruz), R. Bouwens (Leiden University), and the HUDF09 Team (Hubble 'deep field' group of galaxies).
Every effort has been made to trace and acknowledge ownership of copyright. If any rights have been omitted, the publishers offer to rectify this in any subsequent editions following notification.